TExES

Bilingual Target Language Proficiency Test (BTLPT) - Spanish (190)

SECRETS

Study Guide
Your Key to Exam Success

TExES Test Review for the
Texas Examinations of Educator Standards

Dear Future Exam Success Story:

Congratulations on your purchase of our study guide. Our goal in writing our study guide was to cover the content on the test, as well as provide insight into typical test taking mistakes and how to overcome them.

Standardized tests are a key component of being successful, which only increases the importance of doing well in the high-pressure high-stakes environment of test day. How well you do on this test will have a significant impact on your future, and we have the research and practical advice to help you execute on test day.

The product you're reading now is designed to exploit weaknesses in the test itself, and help you avoid the most common errors test takers frequently make.

How to use this study guide

We don't want to waste your time. Our study guide is fast-paced and fluff-free. We suggest going through it a number of times, as repetition is an important part of learning new information and concepts.

First, read through the study guide completely to get a feel for the content and organization. Read the general success strategies first, and then proceed to the content sections. Each tip has been carefully selected for its effectiveness.

Second, read through the study guide again, and take notes in the margins and highlight those sections where you may have a particular weakness.

Finally, bring the manual with you on test day and study it before the exam begins.

Your success is our success

We would be delighted to hear about your success. Send us an email and tell us your story. Thanks for your business and we wish you continued success.

Sincerely,

Mometrix Test Preparation Team

Need more help? Check out our flashcards at: http://MometrixFlashcards.com/TExES

TABLE OF CONTENTS

Top 20 Test Taking Tips

1. Carefully follow all the test registration procedures
2. Know the test directions, duration, topics, question types, how many questions
3. Setup a flexible study schedule at least 3-4 weeks before test day
4. Study during the time of day you are most alert, relaxed, and stress free
5. Maximize your learning style; visual learner use visual study aids, auditory learner use auditory study aids
6. Focus on your weakest knowledge base
7. Find a study partner to review with and help clarify questions
8. Practice, practice, practice
9. Get a good night's sleep; don't try to cram the night before the test
10. Eat a well balanced meal
11. Know the exact physical location of the testing site; drive the route to the site prior to test day
12. Bring a set of ear plugs; the testing center could be noisy
13. Wear comfortable, loose fitting, layered clothing to the testing center; prepare for it to be either cold or hot during the test
14. Bring at least 2 current forms of ID to the testing center
15. Arrive to the test early; be prepared to wait and be patient
16. Eliminate the obviously wrong answer choices, then guess the first remaining choice
17. Pace yourself; don't rush, but keep working and move on if you get stuck
18. Maintain a positive attitude even if the test is going poorly
19. Keep your first answer unless you are positive it is wrong
20. Check your work, don't make a careless mistake

Spelling, Pronunciation, Punctuation, Grammar

Phonetic language

Spanish is a purely phonetic language, which means that every letter, vowels as well as consonants, and combination of letters have their own associated sound. This associated sound is used every single time that this particular letter or combination of letters appears in a word. Therefore, as in all phonetic languages, if you know how to spell a word, you know how to pronounce it. The only exceptions are words adopted from foreign languages. Like in most other language, foreign or nonnative words are sometimes pronounced in Spanish the same way they are pronounced in the original language. In some cases, though, the original pronunciation is modified, and how and in which way it is modified varies by region.

Spanish pronunciation of vowels

Spanish has five vowels, the same as in English, but they are different from English in the sense they have one and only one associated sound regardless of their position in the word and which letters come before and after them. For example, the vowel *a* in Spanish is always pronounced like a shorter version of the *a* in car. There is no difference in the way it sounds whether it is at the beginning of the word (amanecer), between two consonants (caro), between a consonant and a vowel (caer, teatro) or at the end of the word (mesa). In English, though, the vowel *a* has multiple sounds and is pronounced differently in, for example, apple, daughter, day, walk, and also. The same rule applies to *e, i, o,* and *u*: there is only one sound for each of them.

Pronunciation of the letter *r* in Spanish

The letter *r* has two distinctively different pronunciations in Spanish: a soft one, similar to the English *tt* or *dd* sounds (as in jetty or Eddie), and a strong, rolling one. The soft sound is used whenever a single letter *r* is in the middle of a word between two vowels (caro, puro, aire), between a vowel and most consonants (tren, jardín, parte), and at the end of a word (caminar, comer, recibir). At the beginning of a word (reto, rápido, rojo) or after the consonants *l, n,* and *s* (alrededor, sonrisa, Israel), the single letter *r* is pronounced with the trilling sound used in the "double r" or *rr* phoneme.

Pronunciation of the "double r" in Spanish

The "double r" or *rr* is not considered a separate letter, but it is a very frequently used phoneme in Spanish. Some common words that include the *rr* are *correr, perro, arriba, carro*. The *rr* has a trilling sound that can be achieved by flapping the tongue against the front of the mouth. If properly rolled, the *rr* sound should be similar to the one you get when you try to imitate a motor. Be aware that the *rr* is used only between vowels. A similar trilling sound at the beginning of a word or after certain consonants (*l, n, s*) is spelled with a single *r*.

Regional differences in pronunciation of the "double l"

The way the "double l" sounds varies by region, and sometimes even within the same country. In most Spanish speaking areas, the *ll* has a soft sound similar to the English *y* in yes or yellow. In many parts of Argentina and Uruguay, however, the *ll* is much stronger and is pronounced like the *zh* phoneme found in English in words such as measure and pleasure. Common words that have the *ll* phoneme are lluvia (rain), llave (key), llorar (cry), and llegar (arrive).

Pronunciation of the letter *h* in Spanish and English

In English, the letter *h* has a soft, aspirated sound. In Spanish, by contrast, it is always completely silent. Most of the words that contain a letter *h* in Spanish have Latin or Greek roots, and the *h* has been kept just for etymological reasons. The only exceptions to this rule are some foreign words with no equivalent spelling in Spanish such as Hawaii, hamster, and hobby. In those cases, the letter *h* sounds like the Spanish letter *j*. When the letter *h* follows the letter *c* (mucho, chacra, chancho), it forms a new, different phoneme *ch* which has its own particular sound.

Pronunciations of the letter *g* in Spanish

When followed by a consonant (regla, negro) or by the vowels *a*, *o*, or *u* (gaviota, agosto, gusto), the sound of the letter *g* in Spanish is similar to the sound of that same letter in English words, such as good and game. If the letter *g* is followed by the vowels *e* and *i* (generar, registro), the sound of the letter *g* in Spanish is like the sound of the Spanish *j* (a very hard English *h*). If there is a *u* between the letter *g* and the vowels *e* or *i* (guerra, guiso), the letter *g* recovers its soft sound.

Existence of the letter *ñ* in Spanish

The letter *ñ* does not exist in English, and, although it is written as an *n* with a ~ on top, it is completely distinct from the letter *n*. In Spanish, it can be found in words such as mañana (morning or tomorrow), año (year), señor (mister), niña (girl), etc. The most similar sounds in English that resemble the *ñ* in Spanish are the *ny* or *ni* phonemes as found in words such as canyon, onion, or opinion, but pronounced fairly stronger. In the Spanish alphabet the *ñ* is located after the letter *n*.

Pronunciation of the letter *y* in Spanish

In Spanish, the letter *y* is treated as a vowel. At the end of a word (rey, muy, soy), it is always pronounce as the vowel *i*. If the letter *y* is before a vowel (yo, ya, yarda), in most countries it is also pronounced as the vowel *i*. However, in Argentina and Uruguay, the letter *y* before another vowel sounds more like the *sh* English phoneme as found in words such as shower and show.

Pronunciation of the letter *ch* in Spanish and English

The Spanish *ch* is different from English in the sense that it is always pronounced the same way. It has the exact same sound as found in English words such as church, charcoal, and march. Spanish dictionaries have a separate section for the *ch*, and it is located after the letter *c*. Common words in Spanish with *ch* are chancho, chispa, chino, chaqueta, etc.

Pronunciation of the "double c" in Spanish

Occidente, collección, and diccionario are some words in Spanish that use the "double c" or *cc*. In this phoneme, the first *c* has the strong sound of an English *k*, while the second *c* is much softer and has the same sound as an *s*. Overall, the *cc* sounds mostly like the same combination of letters sound in English in words such as accident and access, or like the *x* sound found in x-ray and excess.

Letter *w* in Spanish

The letter *w* is not native to the Spanish language, and it appears only in words that come from other languages. Depending on the country, it is called "uve doble," "v doble," "doble u," or "doble v." Words in Spanish with a *w* have mostly English roots (waterpolo, hawaiano, whisky) and are usually pronounced with the English *w* sound as found in water, when, winter, etc. In some countries, however, the *w* is pronounced with a very soft *g* added before the English *w* for a *gu* sound.

Pronunciation of the letter *j* in Spanish

The letter *j* has a completely different pronunciation from that of the same letter in English. Actually, the sound of the Spanish *j* does not exist in English. The closest sound would be an extremely hard and strong *h*, an exaggeration of the sound in words such as hot and home. In some regions, the *j* is pronounced slightly softer but it still is much harder than the English *h*. Be aware that in Spanish, the letter *g*, when followed by the vowels *e* as in género and digerir or *i* as in registrar and higiene, has the same strong sound as the letter *j*.

Pronunciations of the letter *c* in Spanish

The letter *c* has two different pronunciations depending on which letter is after it, much as it is in English. If followed by an *a* (camino), *o* (correr), *u* (cuñado), or a consonant (conectar), the letter *c* sounds like the English hard *c* in come and camera or the *k* in break and kimono. If followed by the vowels *e* (centro) or *i* (cigarillo), the letter *c* sounds like the *c* in face and celery. In some countries, Spain for example, the *s* sound of the letter *c* is much softer, almost like the sound of the letter *z*. Note that in the particular case of the letter *c* followed by the consonant *h* (chico), it forms the new letter *ch*, which has a similar sound as the English *ch* in church.

Spelling of the phoneme *f* in English and Spanish

The sound of the phoneme *f* in Spanish is the same as the sound of that phoneme in English as found in words such as family and future. It is never pronounced with the *v* sound found in *of* for example. Another major difference is that the phoneme *f* is obtained in Spanish only by the use of the letter *f*, while in English the same sound appears in words with *f* (face), *ff* (coffin), and *ph* (photograph). The letter *f* is never doubled and the *ph* combination does not exist in Spanish. In some foreign words the *ph* has been replaced by a single *f* (telephone–teléfono, photograph-fotografía).

Letter *q* in Spanish

In Spanish, the letter *q* has the sound of the English letter *k*. The letter *q* is always followed by a *u* (*qu*) and then either an *e* (querido, quebrar, quemar, quedar, quejido) or an *i* (quizá, quitar, quince, quirúrgico, quieto). There are very few exceptions (quantum, quorum) and they all have foreign roots.

Letter *z* in Spanish

In Spanish the letter *z*, regardless of which letter comes after it, has the same sound as the letter *c* before an *e* (centauro) or *i* (cocina). Therefore, in most of Latin America countries, it sounds like the *s* in English words such as silence and serious, while in most of Spain it sounds like the *th* in English words such as think and thunder. In Spanish, the letter *z* cannot be used before an *e* or *i* except in words of foreign origin (zepelin, zigzaguear). Due to this rule, the letter *z* is replaced by a *c* when forming the plural of words ending in *z* (lápiz/lápices, tapiz/tapices).

Rules for the written stress or accent mark

The Spanish language uses a written stress or accent mark on vowels to denote exceptions to its stressing rules. Words with a stress in the last syllable will have a written stress or accent mark if they end in a vowel (mamá, café, así) or the consonants *n* (camión, común, jamón) or *s* (jamás, francés, anís). For those words stressed in the second-to-last syllable, an accent mark is needed when they end in any consonant (ángel, álbum, cadáver, lápiz) except *n* and *s*. For words stressed in the third-to-last syllable, a written stress is always required, regardless of the last letter (apéndice, códigos, diplomático).

There are a few special rules when it comes to the written stress or accent mark in Spanish:
- One-syllable words never have a written accent except when there are two possible different meanings: el (the) and él (he), si (if) and sí (yes), tu (your) and tú (you), mas (but) and más (more).
- Some two-syllable words that might have two possible different meanings or functions in the sentence: solo (alone) and sólo (only), este (demonstrative adjective as in yo leo este libro/I read this book) and éste (demonstrative pronoun as in éste es mi libro/this is my book).
- Adverbs such as cuándo (when), dónde (where), and cómo (how) as well as pronouns such as quién (who), qué (what), and cuál (which) require an accent mark when used in questions and interrogatory sentences.

Capitalization

Capitalization is not used in Spanish as much as in English. The first word of a sentence is always capitalized. Proper names of people (Jorge Luis Borges, María), companies (Sony, Chevron) and places (España, Madrid, el río Nilo) are capitalized. Abbreviations of personal titles (Sr., Dr.) are capitalized but, if the full word is used, it is written in small case (el señor Aguilar, el doctor Fuentes). For titles of books, stories, poems, essays, songs, films, etc., only the first word is capitalized (La Guerra de las galaxias). The days of the week (lunes, viernes) and the months of the year (enero, abril) are not capitalized. Nationalities (argentino, australiano) and languages (latín, inglés) are not either.

Writing dates

In Spanish the days of the week and the months of the year are not capitalized unless they are at the beginning of a sentence. The proper way to write a date is 18 de diciembre de 1948 in contrast to the usual format of December 18, 1948 in English. However, the form diciembre 18, 1948 has started to show up in some places. When using dashes or slashes, the order is not the same: in English it is month/day/year while in Spanish is day/month/year. The correct meaning is obvious in some instance. There is no doubt that 25/12/2012 means December 25, 2012 as there is no 25th month. But in some cases it can be confusing. 3/7/2012 is July 3, 2012 in Spanish and March 7, 2012 in English. Be aware of this difference when reading and writing.

Writing numbers

The English language uses a period to denote the decimal point in a number and commas every 3 digits. In the Spanish language, it is just the opposite: a comma is used to denote the decimals and periods are used every 3 digits. The value of a penny would be written as 0.01 of a dollar in English and 0,01 of a dollar in Spanish. The number ten thousand will be written in English as 10,000, while in Spanish it will be 10.000. When writing or reading a definite number, the words hundred, thousand, and million in English are always in singular. In Spanish, the words cien and millón use the singular or the plural form in accordance with the number, while the word mil is always in singular (200 = doscientos; 1.000.000 = un millón, 5.000.000 = cinco millones; 3000 = tres mil).

Special Interrogation and exclamation marks

In Spanish, as in English, questions end with the interrogation mark (?), and exclamations end with the exclamation mark (!). But in Spanish for both types of sentences an inverted mark is require at the beginning. Therefore, all questions in Spanish begin with ¿, and all exclamations begin with ¡. Computer keyboards for the English language do not have a key for these symbols, and there are different options you can use to insert them depending on the program you are using. Familiarize yourself with the particular option you will have to use in the test.

Interrogative form

The structure of sentences denoting interrogation is very much the same in English and in Spanish. If the questions include interrogative adjectives, pronouns and adverbs such as quién, cuál, cómo, etc., the questions begins with those words (¿Quién vino?, ¿Cuál es tu casa?, ¿Cómo estás?). In all other cases the question will begin with the verb followed by the subject, as it is done in English (¿Llegaron los niños de la escuela?). Be aware that many times the subject is included in the verb and not specified otherwise (¿Llegaron de la escuela?). In their interrogative form, the interrogative adjectives, pronouns, and adverbs mentioned above always have a written stress or accent mark. Questions in Spanish require an interrogation mark at the beginning (¿) as well as at the end (?).

Exclamatory form

Exclamations in Spanish are usually expressed with qué in a very similar manner as English does with what (¡Qué día tan bonito!/What a beautiful day!) and how (¡Qué bonito!/How beautiful!). The exclamatory form is also use to denote a warning (¡Cuidado!/Careful!), an order (¡No hable!/Don't talk!) and emotions (¡Por fin llegaste!/You finally arrived!) in the same way as the English language does. As with interrogative adjectives, pronouns and adverbs such as qué, cómo, cuánto, etc., have a written stress or accent mark. In Spanish, also, all exclamations require an exclamation mark (¡) at the beginning as well as at the end (!).

Special cases for the spelling of conjunctions

For phonetic reasons, the conjunction y (and) changes to e when the word after the conjunction starts with i or hi (español e inglés, padre e hijo, Susana e Isabel). Something similar occurs with the conjunction o (or), which is changed to u when the word that follows it starts with o or ho (setenta u ochenta, casas u hoteles, Carlos u Honorio). When the conjunction but (pero) introduces a positive phrase that is contrary to the negative statement that precedes the conjunction, the conjunction used is sino (no quiero vino sino cerveza, no me gustan los perros sino los gatos, no hablamos con el director sino con su secretaria).

Changes in spelling for verbs ending in -uir

Verbs ending in -uir (incluir, huir, construir, contribuir, destruir) have a y in the present tense (yo incluyo, tú huyes, él construye, ellos contribuyen) before all endings except those beginning with an i (nosotros destruímos). The same rule applies for the past tense (él construyó, ellos contibuyeron, nosotros destruímos). The letter y in these words is pronounced like an i, except In Argentina and Uruguay where its sound is closer to the sh sound in English.

Spelling changes in verbs ending in -cer and -cir

Verbs in Spanish that end in -cer (conocer, parecer, merecer, ofrecer, crecer) or -cir (conducir, lucir, traducir, producir) preceded by a vowel are irregular in the present tense of the indicative for the first person singular yo. These verbs have -zco as the ending for that particular tense and person (yo conozco, yo ofrezco, yo crezco, yo conduzco, yo traduzco, yo produzco). Similarly, in the present of the subjunctive tense, for all persons , these verbs use the ending -zca (que el merezca, que ellos aparezcan, que nosotros luzcamos). The same rules apply to all other verbs derived from those mentioned above (desconocer, desaparecer, aparecer, desmerecer, deslucir).

Spelling changes in verbs ending in -gar

The letter g in Spanish has always a hard sound before a (garúa), o (cargo), and u (gusano) but a soft sound before e (coger) and i (régimen). In those verbs ending in -gar (jugar, pagar, llegar), in order to keep the hard sound of the letter g, a u is added after the g for the first person singular form of the past tense (yo jugué, yo pagué, yo llegué), as well as in some subjunctive and imperative forms (jueguen, paguemos).

Spelling changes in verbs ending in -car

In Spanish, the letter c has a hard sound, like the letter k in English, when is it followed by an a (carro), o (colegio), or u (curva), and a soft sound like the c found in English in words

- 7 -

Handwritten notes at top:

Car → subj & Past
qu

such as century and cigar, when it is followed by the vowels *e* (celoso) or *i* (cien). To keep the hard sound of the letter *c* in the first person singular of the past tense of verbs ending in -car (sacar, tocar, buscar), the letter *c* is replaced by *qu* (yo saqué, yo toque, yo busqué) as well as in most subjunctive and imperative forms (toquemos, ¡no saques!).

Spelling changes in verbs ending in -ger and -gir

Handwritten: Present j → a - o - u

The letter *g* in Spanish always has a hard sound like the same letter in English in words such as garnet and gray before the letters *a* (gaviota), *o* (govierno), and *u* (agudo), but a soft sound before *e* (gerente) and *i* (agitar). In those verbs ending in -ger (escoger, recoger) and -gir (elegir, dirigir), to keep the soft sound for the first person singular in the present tense, the letter *g* is replaced by the letter *j*, which always has a soft sound (yo escojo, yo recojo, yo elijo, yo dirijo), as well as in all present subjunctive forms (que tú recojas, que elijamos), and negative commands (no elijas, no escojan).

Handwritten: Past subj ce - cen

Spelling changes in verbs ending in -zar

In Spanish, the letter *z* is never used before *e* or *i*; the letter *c* is used instead. Therefore verbs ending in -zar (empezar, alcanzar, utilizar), the *z* is replaced by a *c* for any conjugation ending in *e* (yo empecé, no alcances, que uds. utilicen). Also, because of this rule, there are no verbs ending in –zer or -zir.

Gender in Spanish words

There are two genders in Spanish, masculine and feminine, for nouns, adjectives, and articles. Every noun has a gender. There is no neutral (like *it* in English), and inanimate objects and other nouns that define similar concepts have a gender. There are no rules to determine which gender is assigned to each noun. With some exceptions, nouns that end with the letter *o* are masculine (carro, libro), and nouns that end with the letter *a* are feminine (casa, mesa). Nouns that refer to people or animals generally have the two versions: one ending in *a* for the female (niña, gata, perra), and one ending in *o* for the male (niño, gato, perro). Sometimes, as in English, the female and male of the same animated object use different nouns (woman/man, mujer/hombre) but the gender assignment is consistent with the gender they represent. The same rules apply to adjectives (casa cara/expensive house, libro caro/expensive book) and articles (las calles/the streets, los lápices/the pencils).

Word order in sentences

Both English and Spanish are basically SVO languages: languages in which the more common sentence structure is Subject + Verb + Object (The boy eats bread/El niño come pan). English is more structured and allows variations in word order mainly only for questions or in literature. Spanish is more flexible, and it is very common to find sentences where the verb or the object is at the beginning of the sentence (Pedro leyó este libro/Leyó Pedro este libro/Este libro lo leyó Pedro). The meaning of the sentence remains basically the same but with some subtle variations on emphasis. It is important to remark also that very often the subject is included in the verb in Spanish (Llegamos tarde/We arrived late).

Word derivatives

A derivate word is one that has been formed using an existing word as the basis. Derivatives are not variations of a word, like different conjugation forms of the same verb (eat/eats/eating) but new words (clear/clearly/unclear, respect/respectful/disrespect). The concept is the same in Spanish (persona/personalmente/impersonal, conocer/conocimiento/desconocer). In many cases, similar rules apply to English and Spanish. For example, deriving an adjective from an English noun ending in -tion by adding --al (recreation/recreational) is equivalent to replacing the -ción ending in a Spanish noun with -tivo to form an adjective (recreación/recreativo). Knowing the concept and the rules of derivation in Spanish is very useful to improve listening and comprehension skills, expand vocabulary, and increase fluency in the target language.

Instances where the same word is used both in Spanish and in English

All languages incorporate words and phrases from other languages. Spanish and English are no exceptions. English words related to technology have crossed over to a wide range of languages and words like e-mail, click, and DVD, for example, have been absorbed into Spanish, becoming a part of it. Spanish words have made their way into English, too. For some of them there is a translation (bodega/grocery store, fiesta/party, patio/courtyard), but many have no equivalent in English (adobe, armadillo, tango). Both languages also share the use of some French words (amateur, ballet, boulevard). Examples of loan words from Italian used both in English and Spanish include many musical terms (aria, cadenza, opera, piano, viola). And many of the words borrowed from German are used in philosophy in Spanish and in English (angst, ersatz, gestalt, geist).

Formal and informal forms of address

In English, there is only one second-person singular pronoun, you, for both formal and informal ways of addressing people. In Spanish, there are two forms: the formal usted and the informal tú. The informal tú has its own particular conjugation for all tenses (tú vienes, tú fuiste, tú comerás, tú has dormido). The informal tú also has its own set of possessive and reflexive pronouns (tu libro, tus hermanos, esta casa es tuya, Ana te invite al concierto). The formal usted, on the other hand, uses the same verb conjugations as the third-person singular pronoun él (usted viene, usted comerá, usted ha dormido). In a similar way, usted uses the third-person singular possessive and reflexive pronouns (su libro, sus hermanas, esta casa es suya, Ana lo invitó al concierto). In much of the Spanish speaking world, the second-person plural form for both formal and informal uses is ustedes, which shares its verb forms with ellos/ellas (ustedes tienen, ustedes vendrán, ustedes han comido). A few areas (such as Spain) differentiate between the formal and informal second-person plural, using ustedes formally , and vosotros informally (vosotros habláis, vosotros habéis visto, vosotros comisteis).

Vos as an informal form of address

In some areas of the world, such as Argentina and Bolivia, the informal second-person singular pronoun tú is very seldom used. Instead, these countries use vos. Vos has its own conjugations. For most tenses, these conjugations are the same as those of tú (tú comiste/vos comiste, tú has ido/vos has ido, tú comprarás/vos comprarás). The conjugations for vos are almost always different in the present indicative. In the case of regular verbs, the conjugation for vos is usually the same as tú, but with the stress on the last syllable (tú comes/vos comés, tú llegas/vos llegás). Exceptions abound with irregular verbs: tú vienes/vos venís, tú eres/vos sos, tú cierras/vos cerrás.

Conocer and saber

There are two different verbs in Spanish, that correspond to the infinitive phrase *to know* in English, conocer and saber. Saber is used when to know implies a mental effort, study, or training (she knows how to cook pasta/ella sabe cocinar pasta, he knows the lesson/él sabe la lección, they know to get to the school/ellos saben como llegar a la escuela). Conocer is used when to know denotes knowing through familiarity or acquaintance (he knows Mr. Jones/él conoce al Sr. Jones, she knows this part of the city/ella conoce esta parte de la ciudad).

Parecer

The verb parecer has different meanings in Spanish depending on whether it is used as a nonreflexive or reflexive verb. When used as a nonreflexive verb, it means to appear/to seem and expresses some level of uncertainty (el niño parece estar enfermo/the boy appears to be sick, parece que va a llover/it seems it is going to rain). Used as the reflexive verb parecerse, it means to resemble (Elena se parece a su hermano/Elena resembles her brother, dicen que yo me parezco mucho a mi padre/they say I resemble my father a lot).

Infinitive form

In English, the infinitive form of a verb is denoted by the marker *to* that precedes it. In Spanish, no marker precedes an infinitive, and the infinitive form is denoted by the endings ar (caminar, llorar, estar), er (correr, vender, ser), or ir (escribir, decir, ir). Each group has its own conjugation forms for all tenses, and they apply to all regular verbs that belong to that particular conjugation. Conjugated forms for irregular verbs vary from group to group and even within the same conjugation.

Expression hace…que

To describe an action that starts in the past and continues in the present, the Spanish language uses the present perfect tense (yo he estudiado español un año, Juan ha esperado dos horas, nosotros hemos vivido en esta ciudad muchos meses). Very often, these same type of ideas is expressed with hace …que, which can be compared to the it's been in English (hace un año que yo estudio español, hace dos hora que Juan espera, hace muchos meses que nosotros vivimos en esta ciudad). When using hace…que, the sentence begins with hace, the time modifier, and then que, followed by the subject and verb, which is no longer in the present perfect of the indicative.

The verb haber:

	yo	tú	él	nosotros	ustedes	ellos
indicative present	he	has	ha	hemos	habéis	han
indicative imperfect	había	habías	había	habíamos	habíais	habían
indicative preterit	hube	hubiste	hubo	hubimos	hubisteis	hubieron
future	habré	habrás	habrá	habremos	habréis	habrán
conditional	habría	habrías	habría	habríamos	habríais	habrían
subjunctive present	haya	hayas	haya	hayamos	hayáis	hayan
subjunctive imperfect	hubiera/ hubiese	hubiera/ hubieses	hubiera/ hubiese	hubiéramos/ hubiésemos	hubierais/ hubieseis	hubieran/ hubiesen

In Spanish, the auxiliary verb used to form all perfect tenses is haber. It is an extremely irregular verb and has two different, interchangeable forms (hubiera/hubiese) for the imperfect of the subjunctive. Due to its importance as an auxiliary verb, all of its forms should be mastered. Haber is also used to form the past tense of deber (must) (John must have gone to the theater with Mary/John debe haber ido al teatro con Mary) and debía (should) (You should have called Susan last night/tú deberías haber llamado a Susan anoche) in those clauses that express probability. See the table on the opposite side for the conjugation of haber.

Quisiera

Quisiera and other forms of the imperfect subjunctive of querer are used very often in Spanish followed by an infinitive to express a polite request or desire and to soften a statement (yo quisiera hablar con usted, nosotros quisiéramos visitor Francia). It can be compared to "would like" in English (I would like to talk with you, we would like to visit France). If a different subject is introduced after quisiera (yo quisiera que usted...), then an infinitive clause cannot be used, and it must be replaced by a subordinate clause that uses the imperfect of the subjunctive (yo quisiera que usted me acompañara, Juan quisiera que el trabajo fuera más fácil).

Position of pronouns when using the present participle

The personal pronouns me, te, le, lo, la, nos, les, los, and las, when used as direct or indirect objects of a present participle are attached to the end of the present participle to form a single word (escribiéndome, escuchándote, mirándola, siguiéndonos). In the case of the progressive tenses with estar, there are two different and correct forms commonly used: the pronoun object can either be before the present participle as a separate word (Pedro me estaba diciendo, José te estaba leyendo el diario, Susana nos estaba esperando) or attached to the end of the participle (Pedro estaba esperándome, José estaba leyéndote el diario, Susana estaba esperándonos).

Reflexive verbs instead of the passive voice

The reflexive form of a verb is very commonly used in Spanish instead of the passive voice in those cases where the subject of the sentence is an inanimate object or when the

- 11 -

performer of the action is not important or is not specified. This particular structure is more often used in the present tense. For example: *se vende carne en esa tienda* instead of *carne es vendida en esa tienda*; *se espera una gran lluvia* instead of *una gran lluvia es esperada*; *¿cómo se dice en español "grocery store"?* instead of *¿cómo es dicho "grocery store" en español?*

Most common reflexive verbs that have a different meaning in Spanish

There are several verbs in Spanish that have a different meaning, depending on whether they are used as reflexives verb or not. Parecer means to seem or to appear (parece que va a llover/it seems it is going to rain) while parecerse means to resemble (Juan se parece a su padres/Juan resembles his father). Dormir means to sleep (Ana duerme ocho horas por día/Ana sleeps eight hours per day) while dormirse means to fall asleep (Jorge se durmió en el tren/Jorge fell asleep in the train). Other examples are llamar (to call) and llamarse (to be named) and llevar (to carry) and llevarse (to get along).

Ojalá

hope + subj

The Spanish word ojalá does not have an exact translation in English. It is used to express a wish (ojalá supiera nadar/I wish I knew how to swim) or hope (ojalá que mañana sea un lindo día así podemos ir a la parque/I hope that tomorrow is a nice day so we can go to the park). In these cases, the world ojalá is always followed by the subjunctive (ojalá hubiera sabido esto ayer; ojalá lleguemos a tiempo; ojalá aprobemos el examen; ojalá hubiéramos salido más temprano).

Distributive adjectives and pronouns

cada - todos - todo

While in English there are usually two different distributive adjectives and pronouns with the same meaning (each and every, everyone and everybody), in Spanish there is only one form for each particular connotation. Each and every are translated as cada (each season has its advantages/cada estación tiene sus ventajas; every passenger carried his suitcase/cada pasajero cargaba su maleta). The equivalent of everyone and everybody is todos (everyone loves him/todos lo aman; everybody was ready/todos estaban listos) and everything is todo (everything he said was true/todo lo que dijo era verdad).

Compound relative pronouns and the subjunctive

quienquiera
dondequiera, que + subj
cualquiera

The compound relative pronouns quienquiera (whoever), cualquiera (whatever/whichever), and dondequiera (wherever) are always followed by que and then the verb in the subjunctive mode: quienquiera que escuche este sermon será transformado/whoever listens to this sermon will be transformed; este libro es útil para quienquiera que lo lea/this book is useful to whoever reads it; cualquiera que sea la causa, el resultado será el mismo/whatever the cause is, the result will be the same; dondequiera que él vaya, lo encontraremos/wherever he goes we will find him).

Different kinds of adverbs

Both in English and in Spanish, adverbs modify verbs, adjectives, other adverbs, and clauses (the bird flew high/el pájaro voló alto; the mountain is very high/la montaña es muy alta; the student knew the topic quite well/el estudiante sabía el tema bastante bien) in the same way adjectives modify nouns (it is a high mountain/es una montaña alta). There are several kinds of adverbs:

- of manner: rápidamente (quickly), bien (well), apropiadamente (appropriately)
- of place: aquí (here), allá (there), alrededor (around)
- of time: ahora (now), pronto (soon), hoy (today)
- of frequency: nunca (never), ocasionalmente (occasionally), a menudo (often)
- of degree: muy (very), bastante (quite), demasiado (too)
- interrogative: cuándo (when?), dónde (where?), por qué (why?)
- relative: cuando (when), donde (where), por que (why)

Equivalents in Spanish of Neither...nor and either...or

Spanish does not have two different words to express a combination of two alternative things. In the case of a negative connotation, it uses *ni* for both conjunctions neither and nor (neither the father nor the son are blond/ni el padre ni el hijo son rubios). Similarly, for affirmative or interrogative sentences, the Spanish language only uses *o* for both conjunctions either and or, (we can eat either meat or fish/podemos comer o carne o pescado; can I take either the train or the plane to go to Chicago?/¿puedo tomar o el tren o el avión para ir a Chicago?)

Equivalents in Spanish of some and any

In English, there are two different words to express the concept of a certain amount: some, which is used in affirmative sentences (we have some time), and any, which is used in negative and interrogative sentences (we don't have any ideas; do you have any brothers?). The Spanish language uses algún (alguna, algunos, algunas) o un poco de (tenemos algún/un poco de tiempo; ¿tienes algún hermano?) for affirmative and interrogative sentences, and ningún (ninguna, ningunos, ningunas) or nada de for negative sentences (no tenemos ninguna idea; no tenemos nada de cambio). The same rule applies to compound words formed with some and any. Spanish will use alguien (somebody/anybody), algo (something/anything), algún lugar (somewhere/anywhere, etc.) for the affirmative and interrogative forms, and nadie, nada, ningún lugar, etc., for the negative form.

Equivalents in Spanish of many/much and few/little

In English, many is used before countable nouns (many books, many things), and much before uncountable nouns (much money, much meat). The Spanish language does not differentiate between countable and uncountable nouns and uses only the word mucho. However, the ending of mucho will change according to the gender and number of the noun that follows (muchos libros, muchas cosas, mucho dinero, mucha carne). The same thing happens with few (few mistakes, few houses) and little (little time, little milk). In both cases they will be translated as poco, whose ending will agree in gender and number with the noun that follows (pocos errors, pocas casas, poco tiempo, poca leche).

Definite article

There is only one definite article in English, the, used to refer to something in a general way. It does not denote quantity or gender, being the same for singular, plural, feminine, and masculine nouns. By contrast, Spanish has different forms or variations depending on the characteristics of the noun. The masculine, singular form is el. The masculine, plural form is los. The feminine, singular form is la. The feminine, plural form is las. The definite article must always be in agreement in number and gender with the noun it precedes (el libro, la revista, los cigarros, las zanahorias). The definite article el does not have a written accent. When written with a stress mark, the word has a different meaning (él/he).

Conditional tense
[handwritten: if + subjunctive / verb-ría]

The conditional tense in Spanish is used in the same way the conditional is used in English:
- with the subjunctive in true conditional if clauses (si yo fuera Juan, no iría a la fiesta/if I were Juan, I wouldn't go to the party; si lloviera, el jardín no se vería tan feo/if it rained, the garden wouldn't look so ugly)
- in indirect speech, when the main verb is in the past and the second verb denotes a future action in the past (Juan dijo que hablaría con ella/Juan said he would talk with her; Pedro me informó que iría al cine/Pedro informed me he would go to the movies)

[handwritten: Libro = Librito]

Diminutives
[handwritten: α + ito / α + ita]

Diminutives are used to denote smallness or to express affection, and are usually formed in Spanish by adding the suffix ito at the end of the noun. If the noun ends in an unaccented vowel, the vowel is dropped (libro/librito; perro/perrito). If the noun ends in e, n, or r, a c is added to the suffix (padre/padrecito; joven/jovencito; mujer/mujercita). The suffix has to agree with the gender and number of the noun (camión/camioncito; collares/collarcitos; blusa/blusita; silla/sillitas). Other spelling changes that need to be taken into account are for nouns that have g or c in the last syllable; they change to gu and qu (lago/laguito; Paco/Paquito).

[handwritten: which / which - where]

Relative pronouns cuyo and donde

The relative pronoun *cuyo* in Spanish is equivalent to whose or of which in English. *Cuyo* has to agree with the gender and number of the noun it modifies, not with the subject that executes the action (la película cuyo director ganó el premio/the movie whose director won the prize; el escritor cuyas novelas leímos en clase/the writer whose novels we read in class).

The relative pronoun donde in Spanish is equivalent to where or which in English and does not have a written accent (la casa donde conocí a Roberto/the house where I met Robert; la puerta por donde salió María/the door through which Mary left).

Conjunctions that sometimes require the subjunctive *[handwritten: (uncertain ideas) comemos donde quieras]*

Some conjunctions such as aunque, como, donde, de manera que, de modo que, según, and mientras, when used to express the opinion of the speaker, uncertainty or a conjecture, require the use of the subjunctive mode (aunque tengamos el dinero, no vamos a comprar un auto nuevo/even though we may have the money—we are not sure we do—we are not going to buy a new car; comemos donde tú quieras/we'll eat where you want—but we do not know where you want to eat). In all other cases, they are followed by the indicative.

Conjunctions that always require the subjunctive

The conjunctions antes (de) que, para que, sin que, a fin de que, a menos que, con tal (de) que, and en caso de que are always followed by the verb in the subjunctive (termina el trabajo antes de que el jefe te lo pida; voy a visitarte para que podamos hablar; hicimos el trabajo sin que ella se diera cuenta; apagué la televisión a fin de que pudieras estudiar; a menos que tengas otra idea, vayamos al cine; con tal de que vengas, no me importa la hora; en caso de que venga el plomero, aquí dejo el dinero para pagarle).

Cognates   *iguales — casi iguales — falsos cognados*

Cognates are words in different languages that have the same etymological origin and similar meaning, spelling, and pronunciation. Some are identical (doctor, terrible, hospital, cruel) and some have minor differences (religion/religión, Canada/Canadá, novel/novela, dentist/dentista, president/presidente, information/ información). Other cognates have larger differences but still have the same root (abandonar/abandon, decidir/decide, universidad/university). False cognates are words that have some similarities in spelling and pronunciation but do not share the same origins and do not have the same meaning (exit/salida—éxito/success, hay/heno—hay/there is, large/grande—largo/long, pie/pastel—pie/foot, rope/soga—ropa /clothes, embarrassed/avergonzada—embarazada/pregnant, fabric/tela—fábrica/factory, library/biblioteca—librería/bookstore).

Possessive adjectives   *mi - tu - su - nuestro*

In Spanish, possessive adjectives refer to the possessor but have to agree also in gender and number with the noun they modify (mi hijo, mis hijos; nuestra casa, nuestras casas). Be aware that Spanish uses the same possessive adjective su for the third person regardless of the gender and number of the possessor (Susan's son—su hijo; Peter's house—su casa; my sisters' books—sus libros; the dogs' food—su comida). Su is also used for the formal second person singular (you brought your book/usted trajo su libro) and for the second person plural (you drink your coffee/ustedes toman su café).

Possessive pronouns   *mío - tuyo - suyo - (replace noun)*

Possessive pronouns in Spanish have the same functions as their English equivalent: they replace a possessive adjective and a noun, and are most commonly used to put emphasis in ownership (the dog is mine/el perro es mío). Possessive pronouns have to be in accordance in gender and number with the noun they are replacing (la casa es nuestra, los libros son tuyos, las sillas son suyas, los lápices son míos). As with the possessive adjectives, the possessive pronoun suyo is used for the third person regardless of gender or number, the formal second person singular, and the second person plural.

The preposition *para*

The prepositions for and to can be translated as *para*. *Para* is used in the following instances:
- Direction or destination (tenemos que salir para la oficina/we have to leave for the office)

- Recipient of something (compré esta blusa para mi hermana/I bought this blouse for my sister)
- Purpose (el plomero vino para arreglar la ducha/the plumber came to fix the shower)
- Time/deadline (siempre vamos a la casa de mis padres para Navidad/we always go to my parents' house for Christmas)
- Comparison (la mesa es demasiado grande para la cocina/the table is too big for the kitchen)
- Intended use (el día es para trabajar/the day is for working)

The preposition *por* *for – per – by – through*

In some instance the preposition for is translated as *por*. *Por* is also used to replace through, by, and per. Por is used in the following instances:
- Means of transportation or communication (lo llamo por teléfono/I call him by phone, voy a Madrid por avión/I go to Madrid by plane)
- Exchange/substitution (cambié la blusa grande por una mediana/I exchanged the large blouse for a medium)
- Duration (los niños jugaron por cuatro horas/the children play for four hours)
- Quantity (ella gana $400 por semana/she earns $400 per week)
- Object of an errand (voy al mercado por la leche/I go to the market for milk)
- Agent (el libro fue escrito por Pedro/the book was written by Pedro)

Demonstrative adjectives *this – that* *este – ese – aquel* (must agree in gender/plural)

In Spanish there are three possible demonstrative adjectives: *este*, *ese*, and *aquel*, compared to the two that exist in English (this, that). *Este* refers to anything close. *Ese* denotes a certain distance. *Aquel* indicates farther away or over there. Demonstrative adjectives, like all adjectives in Spanish, have to agree in gender and number with the nouns they modify (este libro/this book; aquella casa/the house over there; esos gatos/those cats; estas sillas/these chairs).

Demonstrative pronouns *this one – that one* *éste – ése – aquél*

In Spanish there are three possible demonstrative pronouns (éste, ése, aquél) compared to the two that exist in English (this one, that one), and they do not have the word one following them as in English (this one/éste). They have the same form as the demonstrative adjectives (este) but with a written accent (éste). Demonstrative pronouns have to agree in gender and number with the noun they refer to. (blusa—ésta; libro—éste; casas—éstas; perros—éstos). There is also a neutral form (esto, eso, aquello). They do not have a written accent, and they usually refer to ideas or general phrases (¿por qué dices eso?/why do you say that?; no hay nada peor que esto/there is nothing worse than this). *neutral*

Possession

Spanish does not have the 's to express possession. It uses the preposition *de* instead (Tom's book/el libro de Tom; my parents' house/la casa de mis padres). In many instances *de* is followed by the definite article. In those cases, the article has to agree in gender and number with the noun that follows (el libro de la niña; el gato de los vecinos). For phonetic reasons when *de* is followed by *el*, the two words are contracted into *del* (el libro del niño). To inquire about possession, de quién is equivalent to whose (¿de quién es este libro?/whose book is this?). In those cases where you know there is more than one possessor, de quiénes is used in the interrogative form (¿de quienes son estos libros?/whose books are these?). In the interrogative form, there is no difference between feminine and masculine.

Adjectives

[handwritten: After noun / gender / plural]

Adjectives in Spanish have to be in accordance in gender and number with the nouns they modify. Similar rules used to account for gender and number for nouns also apply to adjectives. Adjectives end in *a* for feminine and *o* for masculine (niña bonita/niño bonito). To form the plural an *s* is added to adjectives ending in a vowel (mesa verde/mesas verdes) and *es* (libro azul/libros azules) to those ending in a consonant. Those adjectives ending in *e* use the same form for both genders (casa grande/avión grande). Adjectives are usually put after the noun they modify.

Adjectives that go before the noun

[handwritten: Quantity, Order, Quality → dropp o, a   malo/mal]

In Spanish, adjectives are usually placed after the noun they modify. Exceptions are those adjectives that denote quantity such as *alguno, ambos, bastante, mucho, poco, suficiente, varios* (presentó algunas ideas; ambos estudiantes son alemanes; tengo bastante dinero; hace mucho calor; hay poca comida; tenemos suficiente tiempo; visitamos varias ciudades); and adjectives that refer to order such as *primero, segundo*, etc. (la segunda casa a la derecha). Some adjectives that indicate quality such as *bueno, malo, mejor* and *peor* can be before or after the noun (buena comida/comida buena; el peor caso/el caso peor). In most cases, if the adjective ends in *o*, the *o* is dropped if the adjective precedes the noun (mal libro; buen restaurante; primer piso; algun tiempo).

Adjectives before or after the noun

[handwritten: Change meaning]

Be aware some adjectives have different meanings depending on whether they are before or after the noun they modify. Some examples are:
- la antigua capital/the former capital—la capital antigua/the old capital
- una cierta condición/a certain condition—una condición cierta/a sure condition
- diferentes ideas/various ideas—ideas diferentes/different ideas
- gran universidad/great university—universidad grande/big university
- el mismo jefe/the same boss—el jefe mismo/the boss himself
- pobre hombre/man who deserves pity—hombre pobre/destitute man
- un simple carpintero/just a carpenter—un carpintero simple/a simple carpenter
- la única oportunidad/the only opportunity—la oportunidad única/the unique opportunity

Adverb formation *[handwritten: – mente]*

In Spanish, to form an adverb from an adjective, the suffix *-mente* is added to the feminine, singular form of the adjective (rápido/rápidamente; lento/lentamente). This is similar to the addition of -ly to an adjective to form an adverb in English (quick/quickly; sad/sadly). Adjectives that are the same in the feminine and in the masculine just add *-mente* to its singular form (fácil/fácilmente; triste/tristemente). Adverbs that refer to volume (alto, bajo, fuerte) use the masculine singular and do not add -*mente* (hablar alto). *Demasiado, más, menos, mucho, poco, mejor, peor,* and *tanto* do not change (vayamos más rápido; es el sitio peor iluminado). The adverb that corresponds to *bueno* is *bien*, and to *malo* is *mal* (el hotel está bien ubicado).

Indefinite article   *un / una / unos / unas*

The equivalent of the English indefinite article a/an and its plural some/a few in Spanish is *un*. It has to agree in gender and number with the noun it precedes (un libro, una revista, unos libros, unas revistas). The use of the indefinite article is very similar in both languages, although there are some differences. In general, when talking about religion and profession, there is no need of an indefinite article in Spanish (Pedro es católico/Pedro is a Catholic; Juan es médico/Juan is a doctor) unless an adjective also modifies the noun (Pedro es un católico devoto/Pedro is a devout Catholic; Juan es un médico excelente/Juan is an excellent doctor).

Adverbs and their position in the sentence.   *manner → after verb   V   DO   Adv*

There are some rules regarding the position of an adverb in a sentence:
- adverbs of manner always follow the verb they modify (los chicos jugaron bien el partido)
- adverbs cannot be placed between an auxiliary verb and the principal verb (el hermano ha destruído totalmente el castillo de arena de Paula)
- a direct object is placed between the verb and the adverb (el artista cantó la canción elegantemente)
- when there is more than one adverb ending in -*mente*, only the last one adds it, the other ones use the feminine, singular form of the adjective (me lo explicó claro y completamente)   *>2 adv. → 1 only ends in mente.   fém   mente*

The relative pronoun *que*

Relative pronouns connect two independent sentences. *Que*, which stands for that, who, or whom, is the most common relative pronoun in Spanish. *Que* introduces the relative or dependent clause.

that

Leo un libro. El libro es interesante—El libro que leo es interesante./The book that I read is interesting.

who

Las maestras trabajan en esta escuela. Las maestras son buenas.—Las maestras que trabajan en esta escuela son buenas./The teachers who work in this school are good.

Can not omit que

In English, you can sometimes omit the relative pronoun (the house I like/the house that I like). This omission is not accepted in Spanish (la casa que me gusta).

Nouns and their number

The process to form the plural of a noun from the singular version is very similar in Spanish and English, and consists mainly of adding an *s* at the end of the word. In Spanish, the rule applies to all nouns ending in a vowel (libro/libros; hermana/hermanas). When the noun ends in a consonant, instead of adding an *s*, the noun is pluralized but adding *es*

- 18 -

(mes/meses; ley/leyes; árbol/árboles, pescador/pescadores) just as it is done in English with words that end in s (process/processes). Be aware of required spelling changes when adding *es* (pez/peces; lapiz/lápices).

Nouns, special plurals

Some nouns, such as *anteojos* (glasses) and *tijeras* (scissors), are always used in plural in Spanish. Others, such as *afueras* (outskirts), *ganas* (willingness), and *bienes* (assets), are generally used in the plural but might be occasionally used in the singular. Nouns that have more than one syllable and end with an unstressed vowel plus an *s* do not have a different form for the plural (la crisis/las crisis; el jueves/los jueves; el paraguas/los paraguas). Family names are not pluralized (la familia García vive en esta casa/the García family lives in this house—mi hermana conoce a los García/my sister knows the Garcías)

Agreement

In Spanish, the article and the adjective used with a noun must agree in gender and number with the noun they refer to (el coche rojo, los coches rojos, la blusa amarilla, las blusas amarillas). The subject of the sentence and the verb associated with that subject have to agree in person and number (el niño lloró; los niños lloraron; yo tengo frío; nosotros tenemos frío; tú vienes esta noche; ustedes vienen esta noche). There are also rules for the agreement of verb tenses and modes depending on the type of sentence, especially for conditional phrases (Si Juan se sacara la lotería, él se compraría un coche nuevo).

Nouns and their gender, special rules

There are some special rules regarding the gender of nouns:
- nouns ending in *dad, tad, tud, umbre, ión, ie, cia, ez,* and *eza* are usually feminine (la ciudad, la libertad, la certidumbre, la canción, la serie, la diferencia, la sencillez, la tristeza)
- nouns ending in *aje, ambre, or,* and *án* are usually masculine (el equipaje, el calambre, el valor, el refrán)

Other groups of nouns that are masculine are:
- the days of the week (el martes, el jueves)
- the months of the year (el enero, el agosto)
- languages (el griego, el inglés)
- numbers (el uno, el diez)
- colors (el gris, el blanco)
- infinitives (el contaminar, el caminar)
- rivers, seas, and oceans (el río Nilo, el mar Rojo, el océano Pacífico)

Nouns, other rules to form the feminine

There are some other rules used in Spanish to from the feminine of a noun:
- nouns that end in or, *án, ón,* and *ín* are usually masculine and form the feminine by adding an *a* (doctor/doctora; alemán/alemana; campeón/campeona; bailarín/bailarina).

- nouns ending in *e, ista,* and *nte* stay the same in both the feminine and the masculine forms (el agente/la agente; el artista/la artista; el cantante/la cantante).

Some nouns have the same form for the feminine and the masculine, but their meaning is different depending on the gender (el capital/money—la capital/city; el frente/front—la frente/forehead; el orden/neatness—la orden/command; el policía/policeman—la policía/police force but also policewoman)

Comparison, superiority and inferiority   *más... que*   *menos... que*

In most cases, comparisons in Spanish are denoted by the expressions *más...que* and *menos...que* with the adjective, adverb, or noun placed in between (Juan es más grande que Pedro; yo trabajo más rápidamente que Tomás; tenemos más confianza que tú; mi jardín está menos iluminado que el del vecino; Susana tiene menos dinero que Ana). Some exceptions are *menor* (younger), *mayor* (older), *mejor* (better), and *peor* (worse) (yo soy menor que mi hermano; mi hermano es mayor que yo; Pedro tiene mejor voz que Juan; Juan tiene peor voz que Pedro).

Comparison, equality   Adj *Tan... como*   noun *Tanto... como*

To express a comparison of equality, the Spanish language uses the expression *tan...como* with the adjective or adverb in between (Juan es tan alto como Pedro; Juan escribe tan bien como Pedro). If the comparison includes a noun, the expression *tanto...como* is used (este vaso tiene tanto jugo como ése). In this expression, *tanto* has to agree in gender and number with the noun it refers to (tengo tanto frío como ustedes; Juan tiene tantos juguetes como Pedro; la montaña recibió tanta lluvia como el valle; tengo tantas hermanas como Juan).

Relative superlative   La más / el más / El menos / La menos

The relative superlative applies to a noun in the context of a group. The superlative degree of adjectives in Spanish is expressed by using the comparative form of the adjective (más lindo, menos inteligente) preceded by the definitive article (el más lindo, el menos inteligente). The definite article has to agree in gender and number with the noun it refers to (María es la más bonita de las hermanas; Pedro y Juan son los menos autoritarios del grupo; estas casas son las más caras de la zona). This rule also applies to the irregular comparatives such as *mejor* (best), *peor* (worst), *mayor* (oldest), and *menor* (youngest) (la mejor carne de la región; el peor alumno de la clase, las mayores distancias del país; los menores detalles de la pintura).

Absolute superlative   Muy / extremadamente / ísimo / a

The absolute superlative is the very or extremely in English and does not describe a noun within the context of a group. One way to denote the absolute superlative in Spanish is by adding *muy* or *extremadamente* before the adjective (Pedro es muy inteligente; Juan es extremadamente cuidadoso). Another option is to add the suffix *-ísimo* to the adjective (Pedro es inteligentísimo) in accordance in gender and number with the noun it refers to (ísima, ísimos, ísimas). Adjectives ending in a vowel lose it when the suffix is added (mucho/muchísimo; cara/carísima; malos/malísimos; pequeños/pequeñísimos). Be aware of spelling changes required to comply with spelling rules (rico/riquísimo; largo/larguísimo; feliz/felicísimo).

- 20 -

Gustar

The infinitive *to like* in Spanish requires a different sentence structure than English. In English the word order is the person (subject), the verb, and then the object (I like this book). In Spanish an indirect personal pronoun goes first (representing the person), then the verb, and then the object, which is actually the subject of the sentence (Me gusta este libro). A literal translation of the sentence in English would be: This book is pleasing to me. Other verbs that require the same sentence structure as gustar are: molestar (me molestan los zapatos/the shoes bother me); aburrir (nos aburre la música clasica/classical music bores us); encantar (le encanca cantar/he loves to sing), fascinar; faltar; and interesar.

Ser and estar

Ser and *estar* correspond to the infinitive phrase *to be* in English. *Ser* is used to describe something that is intrinsic to a person, object, or idea, such as nationality (Marta es argentina), origin (la carne es de vaca), identification (Pedro es mi hijo), physical characteristics (soy rubia), generalities (somos estudiantes), dates (hoy es 12 de octubre), time of the day (son las diez de la noche), place of events—where something is occurring—(la fiesta es en mi casa), possession (la casa es mía), and personality traits (Ana es simpática). *Ser* is very irregular; see the table below for its conjugation for the simple tenses of the indicative.

	Present	Imperfect	Preterit
yo	soy	era	fui
tú	eres	eras	fuiste
él	es	era	fue
nosotros	somos	éramos	fuimos
vosotros	sois	erais	fuisteis
ellos	son	eran	fueron

Ser and *estar* correspond to the verb to be in English. Estar is used to describe a condition and sometimes is considered less permanent, about a person, object, or idea. It is used to describe location or position—where something is—(el libro está sobre la mesa; Juan está en Nueva York), physical appearance—i.e. how someone looks— (Susana está bonita con ese vestido), and emotional state (Pedro está contento), as well as actions in progress (María está cocinando; nosotros estamos tomando cerveza). The verb *estar* is very irregular; see the table below for its conjugation for the simple tenses of the indicative.

	Present	Imperfect	Preterit
yo	estoy	estaba	estuve
tú	estás	estabas	estuviste
él	está	estaba	estuvo
nosotros	estamos	estábamos	estuvimos
vosotros	estais	estabais	estuvisteis
ellos	están	estaban	estuvieron

Informal commands

Affirmative commands for *tú* (salta más alto/jump higher) are formed with the present of the indicative conjugation of the third person singular (él salta). When needed, direct personal pronouns can be added at the end of the verb (llámame más tarde/call me later). Be aware that the addition of the pronoun changes the structure of the word and usually requires a written accent or stress mark. Negative informal commands are formed using the present of the subjunctive (no hables tan fuerte/don't talk so loud). *No* is always placed before the verb. Negative informal commands use the direct or indirect personal pronoun as a separate word between *no* and the verb (no me llames esta noche/don't call me tonight).

Past participles

Past participles can be used as adjectives. When used as such, the past participle has to agree in gender and number with the noun it modifies (librería cerrada, consultorio cerrado, tiendas cerradas, edificios cerrados). To form the past participle of regular *–ar* verbs, drop the ending *-ar* and add *-ado* (hablar/hablado); for *–er/-ir* verbs, drop the ending *-er* or *-ir* and add *-ido* (comer/comido, dormir/dormido). *–Er* and *–ir* verbs that have an *a, e,* or *o* before the ending of the infinitive require a written accent in their past participles (caer/caído; sonreir/sonreído; oir/oído).

Irregular verbs with an unexpected *g*

Some verbs have an unexpected *g* in the first person singular of the present of the indicative while they follow the normal conjugation rules for the rest of the forms (hacer/yo hago, tú haces, él hace, nosotros hacemos, ustedes hacen, ellos hacen). Other verbs have the unexpected g but have other irregularities in other persons too (decir/yo digo, tú dices, él dice, nosotros decimos, ustedes dicen, ellos dicen). *Caer, poner, salir, traer,* and *valer* belong to the first group. *Oir, tener, venir*, and their various forms belong to the second group.

Present perfect

The present perfect tense denotes an action in the recent past and is generally used in Spanish the same way it is used in English. It is formed with the present of the indicative of the auxiliary verb haber (yo he, tú has, él ha, nosotros hemos, vosotros habéis, ellos han) and the past participle of the verb (yo he comido bien hoy; tú has viajado a Nueva York este mes; ella ha hecho la tarea esta mañana; nosotros hemos hablado con el director esta semana; ustedes han vivido aquí todo el año; ellos han dormido poco esta noche).

Present indicative

Drop the infinitive ending of the verb and use the endings in the table below to form the present of the indicative for all regular verbs.

	AR	ER	IR
yo	-o	-o	-o
tú	-as	-es	-es
él	-a	-e	-e
nosotros	-amos	-emos	-imos
vosotros	-ais	-eis	-ís
ellos	-an	-en	-en

Examples:
- hablar/yo hablo; caminar/tú caminas; viajar/él viaja; regresar/nosotros regresamos; cepillar/vosotros cepilláis; llamar/ellos llaman
- comer/yo como; aprender/tú aprendes; correr/él corre; desparecer/nosotros desaparecemos; beber/vosotros bebéis; depender/ellos dependen
- vivir/yo vivo; escribir/tú escribes; recibir/él recibe; acudir/nosotros acudimos; batir/vosotros batís; percibir/ellos perciben

The verb *ir*

The verb *ir* is used as an auxiliary verb in Spanish as the "going to" expression in English and to form the continuous tenses (voy a comer a las 2; ellos iban a completar la tarea anoche). The verb *ir* is irregular. See the table below for its conjugation for the simple tenses of the indicative.

	Present	Imperfect	Preterit
yo	voy	iba	fui
tú	vas	ibas	fuiste
él	va	iba	fue
nosotros	vamos	íbamos	fuimos
vosotros	vais	ibais	fuisteis
ellos	van	iban	fueron

El pretérito

Drop the infinitive ending of the verb and use the endings in table below to form the preterit of the indicative for all regular verbs (*-ar, -er,* and *–ir*).

	AR	ER	IR
yo	-é	-í	-í
tú	-aste	-iste	-iste
él	-ó	-ió	-ió
nosotros	-amos	-imos	-imos
vosotros	-asteis	-isteis	-isteis
ellos	-aron	-ieron	-ieron

Examples:
- hablar/yo hablé; caminar/tú caminaste; viajar/él viajó; regresar/nosotros regresamos; cepillar/vosotros cepillasteis; llamar/ellos llamaron
- comer/yo comí; aprender/tú aprendiste; correr/él corrió; desparecer/nosotros desaparecimos; beber/vosotros bebisteis; depender/ellos dependieron
- vivir/yo viví; escribir/tú escribiste; recibir/él recibió; acudir/nosotros acudimos; batir/vosotros batisteis; percibir/ellos percibieron

Imperfect

The imperfect is used to express:
- habitual actions in the past (cuando era niño, siempre jugaba en el parque; siempre íbamos de vacaciones a Canadá)
- age in the past (tenía 9 años cuando conocí a Pedro; ¿cuántos años tenías cuando entraste a la escuela)
- time in the past (¿qué hora era cuando empezó el partido?; eran las nueve de la noche cuando llegué a casa)
- physical and emotional characteristics (Ana era muy alta de niña; mi tío era un hombre muy simpático; Luís estaba muy contento)
- continuous actions interrupted by another action in the past (yo leía una novela cuando sonó el teléfono; Juan dormía cuando empezó el incendio)

Past imperfect

Drop the infinitive ending of the verb and use the endings in the table below to form the preterit of the indicative for all regular verbs.

	AR	ER	IR
yo	-aba	-ía	-ía
tú	-abas	-ías	-ías
él	-aba	-ía	-ía
vosotros	-ábais	-íais	-íais
ustedes	-aban	-ían	-ían
ellos	-aban	-ían	-ían

Examples:
- hablar/yo hablaba; caminar/tú caminabas; viajar/él viajaba; regresar/nosotros regresábamos; cepillar/vosotros cepillábais; llamar/ellos llamaban
- comer/yo comía; aprender/tú aprendías; correr/él corría; desparecer/nosotros desaparecíamos; beber/vosotros bebíais; depender/ellos dependían
- vivir/yo vivía; escribir/tú escribías; recibir/él recibía; acudir/nosotros acudíamos; batir/vosotros batíais; percibir/ellos percibían

Future of the indicative

To form the future of the indicative of all regular verbs, add the endings shown in the table below to the infinitive, regardless of the conjugation -*ar*, -*er*, or -*ir*.

	Future
yo	-é
tú	-ás
él	-á
nosotros	-eremos
vosotros	-éis
ellos	-eran

Examples:
- hablar/yo hablaré; caminar/tú caminarás; viajar/él viajará; regresar/nosotros regresaremos; cepillar/vosotros cepillaréis; llamar/ellos llamarán
- comer/yo comeré; aprender/tú aprenderás; correr/él correrá; desparecer/nosotros desapareceremos; beber/vosotros beberéis; depender/ellos dependerán
- vivir/yo viviré; escribir/tú escribirás; recibir/él recibirá; acudir/nosotros acudiremos; batir/vosotros batiréis; percibir/ellos percibirán

Conditional tense

To form the conditional of all regular verbs, add the endings shown in the table below to the infinitive, regardless of the conjugation -*ar*, -*er*, or -*ir*.

	Conditional
yo	-ía
tú	-ías
él	-ía
nosotros	-íamos
vosotros	-íais
ellos	-ían

Examples:
- hablar/yo hablaría; caminar/tú caminarías; viajar/él viajaría; regresar/nosotros regresaríamos; cepillar/vosotros cepillaríais; llamar/ellos llamarían
- comer/yo comería; aprender/tú aprenderías; correr/él correría; desparecer/nosotros desapareceríamos; beber/vosotros beberíais; depender/ellos dependerían
- vivir/yo viviría; escribir/tú escribirías; recibir/él recibiría; acudir/nosotros acudiríamos; batir/vosotros batiríais; percibir/ellos percibirían

Perfect tenses and their uses

The present perfect is used to denote an action that took place at an indefinite period in the past (yo he leído este libro/I have read this book) or to describe a past action that continues into the present time (hemos vivido aquí muchos años/we have lived here many years).

The past perfect of the indicative is used to denote an action in the past that happened before the second action in the past (cuando me desperté, Marta ya había llegado/when I woke up, Marta had already arrived).

The future perfect is used to denote an action that will be completed in the future before a certain time or another action in the future occurs (me habré graduado antes de ir de vacaciones/I will have graduated before going on vacation).

The conditional perfect is used to denote an action that would have been completed in the past under certain conditions (ella le habría dicho la verdad/she would have told him the truth)

Progressive tenses

Progressive tenses use the verb *estar* as an auxiliary verb with the present participle of the main verb (yo estoy comiendo/I am eating; tú estás durmiendo/you are sleeping; él está estudiando/he is studying; nosotros estamos viniendo/we are coming; vosotros estáis trabajando/you are working; ellos están concinando/they are cooking). The progressive tenses are used to denote an action that is or was in progress (yo estaba durmiendo/I was sleeping; nosotros estuvimos mirando/we were watching). Progressive tenses are never used in reference to the future ("going to" in English). For those cases, Spanish uses *ir a* and the infinitive of the main verb (I am going to do my homework/voy a hacer mi tarea; they are going to finish the book/ellos van a terminar el libro).

Present participle

The present participle (the -ing form in English) is formed in Spanish by dropping the infinitive ending of the verb and adding -*ando* (caminar/caminando; trabajar/trabajando) for –*ar* verbs and -*iendo* for –*er/-ir* verbs (comer/comiendo, correr/corriendo; salir/saliendo; recibir/recibiendo). –*Er/-ir* verbs with irregularities in the present of the indicative usually have an irregular present participle (dormir/durmiendo; creer/creyendo; poder/pudiendo; ir/yendo). The present participle is used in Spanish in largely the same way it is used in English.

Formal commands

Affirmative commands for *usted* (salte más alto/jump higher) are formed with the present of the subjunctive of the third person singular (él hable). When needed, direct/indirect pronouns are added at the end of the verb (llámeme más tarde/call me later, hágalo ahora). Be aware that the addition of the pronoun changes the syllabic structure of the word and requires a written accent or stress mark. Negative informal commands simply add *no* before the verb (no hable tan fuerte/don't talk so loud). *No* is always placed before the verb. Negative formal commands, like informal commands, use the direct/indirect pronoun as a separate word between *no* and the verb (no me llame esta noche/don't call me tonight, no lo haga)

Que and *quien*

Que is used in Spanish as a relative pronoun in reference to persons, objects, and ideas, both for the singular and for the plural (la persona que llamó por teléfono; los niños que jugaban en el parque; los libros que encargué; la admiración que sentía por su padre). If the pronoun is preceded by a preposition, then *quien* must be used instead of *que* when referring to persons (la amiga con quien fui al cine ayer; el hombre a quien ví en la oficina). Sometimes *quien* is used instead of *que* for more clarity (hablé con la maestro nueva, quien estaba muy contenta). *Quien* has to agree in number with its antecedent (las niñas, quienes habían dormido hasta tarde, estaban desayunando)

Cual

In those cases where the use of *que* as a relative pronoun may create confusion or ambiguity, *que* is replace by *el cual* (el primo de mi amigo, el cual vive en Miami, se fue de vacaciones). *El cual* takes the form *la cual, los cuales,* and *las cuales* to agree in gender and number with its antecedent (la mesa, encima de la cual puso las flores, es de madera; ellos tienen cuatro hijos, dos de los cuales viven en Houston; las pinturas, las cuales viste en el museo, se vendieron muy bien). *El cual* is also used after the *prepositions por, sin, después de, además de, contra, detrás,* and *hacia.*

Subjunctive

The subjunctive is used in subordinate clauses introduced by *que* to express:
- a wish (quiero que Juan venga a la fiesta),
- uncertainty or doubt (es probable que María se case con Juan),
- a command (dígale al chofer que esté aquí a las seis),
- an emotion (es una lástima que ustedes no puedan venir a visitarnos),
- preference or need (es mejor que te pongas un abrigo),
- approval/disapproval (está bien que te vistas de negro para el funeral)

The subjunctive is also used with adverbial clauses introduced by the following conjuctions *cuando, antes que, hasta que, tan pronto como, mientras, para que, afin de que, de manera que, sin que, aunque, a menos que,* and *con tal que* (quiero hablar con Pedro tan pronto como llegue; continúen con el trabajo a menos que el jefe diga lo contrario).

Present of the subjunctive

To form the present of the subjunctive of regular verbs, take the first person singular of the present of the indicative (yo hablo), drop the o, and add the endings shown in the table below.

	AR	ER/IR
yo	-e	-a
tú	-es	-as
él	-e	-a
nosotros	-emos	-amos
vosotros	-éis	-áis
ellos	-en	-an

Examples:
- hablar/yo hable; caminar/tú camines; viajar/él viaje; regresar/nosotros regresemos; cepillar/vosotros cepilléis; llamar/ellos llamen
- comer/yo coma; aprender/tú aprendas; correr/él corra; entender/nosotros entendamos; beber/vosotros bebáis; depender/ellos dependan
- vivir/yo viva; escribir/tú escribas; recibir/él reciba; acudir/nosotros acudamos; batir/vosotros batáis; percibir/ellos perciban

Imperfect of the subjunctive

To form the imperfect of the subjunctive of regular verbs, take the third person plural of the preterit of the indicative (ellos hablaron), drop ron, and add the endings shown in the table below.

	AR/ER/IR
yo	-ra
tú	-ras
él	-ra
nosotros	-ramos
vosotros	-rais
ellos	-ran

Examples:
- hablar/yo hablara; caminar/tú caminaras; viajar/él viajara; regresar/nosotros regresáramos; cepillar/vosotros cepillaras; llamar/ellos llamaran
- comer/yo comiera; aprender/tú aprendieras; correr/él corriera; entender/nosotros entendiéramos; beber/vosotros bebierais; depender/ellos dependieran
- vivir/yo viviera; escribir/tú escribieras; recibir/él recibiera; acudir/nosotros acudiéramos; batir/vosotros batierais; percibir/ellos percibieran

Listening, Reading, Writing, Speaking

Knowing beforehand the structure of the test

Familiarize yourself with the structure of test. It is important to know about the different sections of the tests; if the test is timed as whole or by sections; what is the format for the answers (multiple choice, one-sentence answers, one-paragraph answers, a combination of them). For the writing sections, will the test require a minimum and/or a maximum number of words? Also, inquire whether the test will be done on a computer, on paper, or a combination of both. If computerized, make sure your typing skills are up to the task, both in speed and in accuracy, and learn and practice in advance the particular keys you have to use to write those Spanish letters and characters (á, é, í, ó, ú, ñ, ¿, ¡) that do not exist in English.

Importance of timing during tests

Most tests you will take will be timed. Some of them allocate a certain amount of time for the whole test and let you decide how much time you will spend in each section. Others will be more structured and will assign specific time for each section. In both cases, you have to perform a series of tasks (reading, writing, listening, answering multiple-choice or essay questions, etc.) in the time you have been given. It is very important you know how much time you have and how to best use it. Organize yourself: give yourself time to think, to draft, and to review. Do not rush but do not spend too much time on a certain point either. If you see you are running out of time, do not panic; your performance will be better if you stay calm.

Missing a particular word when writing or speaking

Many times you will be writing or speaking and you realize you do not know or do not remember a particular word. Do not panic or try stubbornly to get the word, just go around it. For nouns (percha/hanger), describe what the object looks like (un triángulo con un gancho/a triangle with a hook), what it is made of (alambre/wire, madera/wood, o plástico/or plastic) what it is used for (para colgar la ropa/to hang clothes), or where you can find it (en el armario/in the closet). For adjectives, use opposites. For verbs, use the results of the action. Be sure to convey your message with the proper spelling or pronunciation and in a grammatically correct way.

Steps to follow when answering the written exam

The first step for all writing assignments is to carefully read the instructions, making sure you know what is required in terms of content (the topic), style (formal/informal, narrative/description/etc., letter/essay/etc.), and length (minimum and maximum number of words). It is also important to know how much time you have to complete the section of the test. Once you know what you are required to do, start developing and organizing your ideas. Identify which is the main idea and which are secondary or supporting ideas. Make an outline and do not forget the introduction and the conclusion. Following your outline, write a draft of your answer. Finally, revise your draft. Make sure you have done what was required and it has been presented clearly. To finish, edit for clarity and flow, and proofread for grammar, spelling, and punctuation.

Components of your answers in the written exam

The written part of the test will include a variety of styles and requirements: letters, memos, or e-mails; narrative, descriptive, or opinion texts; formal or informal forms of address. In all cases, your ideas have to be organized and neatly stated. Start by presenting your topic and how you plan to develop it. Continue with the main section of your piece where you tell, describe, or explain your point in a logical manner. Wrap it up by presenting your conclusions and results. The length of these three sections, introduction, body, and conclusion, will depend on the number of words required in your assignment. One or two sentences or a short paragraph are the norm for the introduction and the conclusion.

Elements to consider for the written exam

When completing the written exam, there are certain basic elements that should be taken into consideration. They apply to all writing assignments in all languages. Among them:
- Match answer to assignment (content, style, and length)
- Define your purpose
- Consider your audience
- Select your role and tone
- Develop an outline
- Organize the body of the piece (by space, time, emphasis, or other clustering concept)
- Start with an introduction
- End with a conclusion
- Check for unity and coherence
- Proofread for grammar, spelling, and punctuation

Organizational structures used in the body of a written piece

A well-organized body presents your ideas clearly and efficiently. The organization of the body of your text will depend on the topic, your audience, and your purpose. There are several organizational structures that will cover most situations, among them:
- Spatial, used mainly for descriptions of places, objects, and people
- Chronological, used mostly to narrate events or explain a process
- General to specific, used commonly in discussions
- Climactic (in order of increasing importance), usually arranged from most familiar to least familiar or from simplest to most complex

Outline

The outline is one of the most useful tools to build a clear, well-organized piece. It basically lists your ideas in the order they will be covered. It will guide you through your writing and show the relative importance of each element. An outline can be particularly useful to shape the body of your piece. Create a section of the outline for each main idea. Check the order of the sections. Do they follow the order you want (chronological, spatial, from generic to specific, etc.)? Are all of them relevant? Are there any gaps or overlaps? Within each section, add the secondary ideas and the supporting information and examples. Apply the same questions to the secondary ideas and to supporting material. Reorganize as needed. Once your outline is ready, follow its structure to draft your essay.

Introduction

All writing assignments should begin with an introduction. The topic will be described in the test's instructions, but it has to be presented at the beginning of your text. You cannot assume the reader knows the topic, and you cannot start your piece as a continuation of the instructions. You should also include a brief outline of the main points. The introduction should be simple, clear, and concise. Do not use *el propósito de este ensayo es* (the purpose of this essay is), *estoy escribiendo acerca de* (I am writing about), or similar expressions. The length of the introduction will depend on the total number of words required for the particular assignment. Most of the times, one or two sentences are enough. In other cases, a longer paragraph is more appropriate.

Conclusion

All writing assignments should end with a conclusion. The conclusion will wrap up your piece. It will tell the reader you have finished. It should briefly summarize the main points and might include results or a suggested course of action. Do not restate your introduction and do not include new ideas. Try to avoid expressions such as *aunque no soy experto* (although I am not an expert), *yo creo* (I believe), and *en mi opinión* (in my opinion). The length of the conclusion will depend on the total number of words required for the particular assignment. Most of the time, one or two sentences are enough. In other cases, a longer paragraph is more appropriate.

Identifying patterns in written and oral exams

Asking some questions about the information presented in a written or oral piece and paying attention to specific elements will help you identify what type of text you have in front of you. These questions and elements will also help you when you have to write a specific type of text. Some of the more common options are listed below.
- What happened? → narration
- What does it look, sound, smell, or taste like?→ description
- It includes examples or reasons. → illustration/support
- It is like, or different from, something else. → comparison and contrast
- It happened because… → cause and effect
- What is it? → definition
- It states opinions. → position
- How to do it. → process analysis

Writing process

The writing process consists of three basic stages: development, drafting, and revision. Following these three steps will help you write a well-rounded piece. During the development, you will find and gather information about your topic. You will then select the most relevant information and organize it in an outline. In the drafting stage, you will write your ideas based on the information collected during development, explaining and connecting them. During the revision, you will go through your text, rethinking and rewriting to improve the overall structure and content, editing for clarity and flow, and proofreading for grammar, spelling, and punctuation.

Writing situation

The writing situation refers to your subject and your audience and will help you present the subject to the audience in the most appropriate way. The subject will be provided in the instructions. Make sure you write about what you are required. If the subject is too broad or general, focus on a specific part of the subject, narrowing it to a topic that can be properly addressed in the essay you are writing. In most cases, your audience will be also defined in your assignment. If not, consider the general public with no in-depth knowledge of the particular subject as your audience.

Knowing your audience

Knowing who you are writing for is a very important element for any type of writing assignment. In general, your audience will be defined or implied in the instructions. All good written pieces match the information and the way it is presented to the designated audience. Too much, too detailed, or too specific information may not be appropriate for a general audience. Too general or too little information will not suit a knowledgeable audience. The format and style you use to present the information should also match the audience. Informal, personal sentences are fitting for an e-mail to a friend or family member. A formal tone is required for a letter to a future employer. If you cannot identify your audience from the instructions, consider it as the general public with no in-depth knowledge of your particular subject.

Importance of unity and coherence

Unity and coherence are the two elements that will make a written or oral piece flow smoothly. When checking for unity, see if all parts of the piece support the main idea. All examples and details should be relevant to the central idea. All sections of your piece should relate to each other. If a piece is coherent, the reader/listener will be able to see relations and easily go from one thought to another one. Organize your material in a logical manner. Check for gaps and abrupt transitions and add connective words or phrases to guide the reader along your thinking path.

Revision and editing

It is very important that you have time to revise and edit your written assignments. In this last step, you will be able to correct any mistakes, omissions, or other errors that you overlooked while writing. When revising and editing check that:
- The subject of your piece matches your assignment
- You have answered all questions and included everything that was requested
- You have followed the instructions regarding format
- You have used the appropriate style and tone for your audience
- You have used the right vocabulary and clear and readable language
- Your piece is well-organized
- There are appropriate transitions between paragraphs

- Your grammar is correct
- There are no misspelled words
- You have used the correct punctuation

Summarizing a written or oral piece

You may be asked to summarize a written or oral piece. In doing so, you are being asked to state the same ideas as developed in the piece but in a much more concise form. The amount of information you include in a summary depends on the length allowed for it. Go through the text and find the main ideas. State them as briefly as possible. If you were allotted a small amount of words, the main ideas will be all you can include in the summary. If you still have room, go through the text again and find secondary ideas. Pick up the important ones and include them in the summary, also as briefly and clearly as possible. Make sure you are true to the text. Do not include details and do not add new ideas or your own opinions.

Developing an opinion or position piece

You may be asked to develop a piece based on your own personal opinions about a certain subject. In the introduction, you should start by briefly stating your point of view. The body of the piece should describe your opinion in detail, explaining and justifying it, and refuting any objections. The body should also include examples and material from other sources to support your opinion. Create an outline to make sure your arguments are organized in a clear, logical manner. Avoid using an aggressive tone and attacking other perspectives. Finish the piece restating your opinion and adding possible future actions, if applicable.

Comparison and contrast pieces

Comparison and contrast pieces describe similarities and differences among ideas, people, or things. The introduction should state the subjects and a general description of what features you will compare. For the body, the two most commonly used ways to develop comparisons and contrasts are subject-by-subject and point-by-point. In subject-by-subject, each subject is discussed separately, with a full description of one and then the other. When using this method, keep the order of the elements you compare in the same order for both subjects. In the point-by-point method, the two subjects are discussed at the same time, each element covered for both subject side by side. Examples are usually very useful to clarify ideas in this kind of piece. Finish the piece with your conclusion.

Describing a process

When you explain how to perform a task or how something works, you are describing a process. The first step would be to analyze and fully understand the process. Once familiar with the process you can describe it in a chronological or in spatial way. The method you choose will depend on your subject. Chronologically, you will explain the different steps as they occurred in time, first to last. Spatially, you will organize the information relatively to its physical position (from left to right, for example). For each step, besides defining it and regardless of the method you use, state its purpose and provide any necessary context to make it clear.

- 33 -

Writing memos

A memo (short for memorandum) is usually a short, concise written piece used at work to inform, instruct, or remind about a particular subject. Memos do not have to be very formal, but they do not tend to be very informal either. They must be very clear. The heading of a memo should start with the date, the recipient, and the sender. Include a subject line at the beginning, describing in a few words the topic of the memo (see example of heading below). Use short paragraphs and simple sentences. Include lists and use specific vocabulary. Avoid the passive voice and unnecessary details. Memos do not include a salutation nor signature at the bottom.

MEMORANDUM

July 13, 2012
To: Paul Johnson
From: Lisa Smith

SUBJECT: Personnel changes

Writing e-mails

Nowadays, e-mail is the most common written mode of communication for both personal and business purposes. As with letters, the format and style of an e-mail will depend on the relationship between the sender and the recipient. Family members and friends will use a very informal, colloquial language. E-mails sent to a company asking for a job will be as formal and structured as a letter of inquiry. Read your assignment carefully, and determine how the sender and recipient are related. Use the degree of formality that matches that relationship. Whether formal or informal, organize your thoughts and present them in a clear, logical manner.

Narrations

A narration answers the question, "What happened?" The subject is developed as a story or a sequence of events. The events can be real or fictional. A narration is commonly organized in chronological order, especially in the short pieces you will be asked to write. Narrations are usually written in the first or third person. Since you will be writing about situations that might occur at different times, make sure you use the correct tense for all verbs and that they correlate to the different points in time associated with each action.

Writing descriptions

A description answers the question, "What does it look like?" It can also responds to "What does it smell, sound, taste, or feel like?" A description can be subjective or objective, depending on whether you use your opinions in the essay. A description can be organized relative to space, as from right to left or from top to bottom; from the whole to the parts, as when you describe the general shape of a face and then the eyes, mouth, nose, etc.; or for emphasis, where you start with the most important or relevant traits and then go into other features.

Cause and effect pieces

Cause-and-effect or cause-and-consequence pieces answer basically to the question "Why?" You will analyze and present why something happened or what is likely to happen. It is very important that you keep your ideas very well organized. Do not mix causes and effects. To avoid confusions and misinterpretations, keep as much as possible in the same sentence or paragraph each cause and its effect or consequence and the supporting information. It will be better in most cases also to focus either on the causes or on the effects. Some useful expressions for this type of piece are: *porque, dado que, entonces, así que, debido a, por lo tanto, por eso, por causa de*, etc.

Reading Comprehension questions

During the test, you will be given a passage to read. You will have to answer a series of multiple-choice questions or write an answer based on that text. Read carefully through the passage to grasp and understand its content. Find primary and secondary ideas as well as supporting information and examples. Pay attention to style and tone. Is it written in a formal or a familiar style? Is it polite, authoritarian, or ironic? Is it written in simple or scholarly language? All these elements are cues that you can use to infer information not specifically written in the text but still included in the passage and that will help you better understand the text.

Listening Comprehension questions

During the test, you will listen to a text or conversation. You will have to answer a series of multiple-choice questions or write an answer based on what you heard. Listen carefully throughout the passage to grasp and understand its content. It may help to take notes as you listen. Find the primary and secondary ideas as well as supporting information and examples. Pay attention to style and tone. Is it a formal passage? Does it sound friendly? Does it use simple language? All these elements are cues that you can use to infer information not explicitly stated in the text but still included in the passage. The better you understand the text, the more accurate your answers will be.

Multiple-choice question after reading/listening to a passage

Carefully read/listen to the passage a first time. Read the questions and answer those you are sure about. Make notes about the possible answers to those questions you have doubts about or do not know. Do not spend too much time on any particular question. Read/listen to the passage again, concentrating on finding the missing answers. Go through the questions again and answer them. In most cases, two readings will be enough to complete all questions. If not, reread/listen to the passage and go over the missing answers one more time. Read/listen to the passage one final time. Revise and do a final check on your answers.

Speaking Tasks

The test will include several Speaking Tasks, and you will have some time to prepare for them. During the preparation, make sure that:
- you accurately respond to the content, audience, style, and format requirements
- you present your ideas in an organized, logical manner
- your speech is coherent and has unity (flows smoothly)

- 35 -

- you use the correct words (vocabulary) and grammar

When you deliver your speaking task, make sure that:
- you speak clearly
- you speak neither too fast nor to slow
- you pay close attention to pronunciation

Simulated Conversation section

You might be asked to simulate a conversation in Spanish. You will be given an outline of the conversation. The outline will not give you the exact words that you will hear but just a general idea of what you can expect. You will have a certain time to prepare and deliver your part of the conversation after each line. Listen carefully to the first line of the conversation. Look for the main topic and who the other person is. Pay attention to use of *tú* vs. *usted* and to familiar words and expressions. Note regional cues, educational level of the language, and tone used by the other person. All these elements will help you choose the appropriate content, style, and tone you will use in your answers.

Process to follow for an oral presentation

You may be asked to orally express an opinion on a given topic. You will have some time to prepare your response. Read/listen carefully to the statement defining the topic. List the main points. Explain your opinion, justify it, and refute objections. Support your opinion with examples or by mentioning other available sources. Organize your arguments in a clear, logical manner. Avoid attacking other perspectives. You can finish your presentation by adding possible future actions. When delivering your speech, avoid using an aggressive tone or getting emotional. Speak clearly and not too fast but not too slow either. Pay special attention to your pronunciation.

Listening comprehension, context, tone, and intonation

For the listening comprehension section, it is very important to pay attention to the general context of the narration, description, conversation, or statement. Understanding context is extremely helpful to infer the meaning of words you might not know. It also helps to determine the appropriate meaning for those words that have more than one (*cara*: expensive or face; *frente*: front or forehead). The tone used in an oral piece (happy, serious, ironic, formal) will be another tool to assess the situation. Intonation will help you determine the tense (*hablo* → present and *habló* → past) and if a sentence is an affirmative or a question. Emphasis on particular words will give you clues of what is important (*mi lápiz es azul*/my pencil not my pen; *mi lápiz es azul*/it is blue not red).

Reading comprehension, informative and persuasive styles

When reading a text, it is important to determine the style of the piece. In the informative style, the author presents the information and the data in an objective way. He/she is trying to educate or give something to the audience. On the other hand, in the persuasive style, the writer is trying to convince the reader of his/hers ideas. He/she presents the information from his/her own point of view. In a piece written in the persuasive style, it is important to be able to separate the actual facts from the opinions of the author.

Listening and reading comprehension, main ideas

The first step when reading or listening to a text is to identify the main idea(s) of the piece. In many cases, not everything will be clearly stated. Secondary ideas and supporting examples will help you to infer content within the context of the text. Finding out who the audience is, to whom the piece is intended, and the style and tone of the text will give a more accurate indication of the purpose of the material. It is also important to pay attention to the sequence of events and to cause-and-effect relationships to be able to answer questions properly.

Practice Test

Practice Test

Section 1 – Listening and Cultural Knowledge

In the listening section of the test you will hear several texts, dialogues and conversations recorded by native Spanish speakers; you will then have to answer multiple choice questions based on the material you have heard. With so many Spanish speaking countries, each one with its own particular accent, expressions, and vocabulary, you will have to listen carefully as the pronunciations will differ, and there may be different words and phrases to describe the same object, action or quality. You will listen to each selection twice, with a brief break between them to look at the questions. After the second time, the questions will be shown on the screen one by one. You will have to answer them as they come up, and you will not be able to go back.

The selections are real spoken language; therefore they will vary in structure, delivery and content. They can be chats, interviews, dialogues and other oral interactive exchanges of two or more people. They can also be presentations, lectures, or readings by only one speaker. They can be formal or informal; it can be a cultured delivery or just a plain, everyday conversation. The speakers may talk slowly and clearly, fast and linking words, or hesitantly and with pauses and repetitions. There may be background noise too (cars, other people talking or music). As for content, the topics are endless.

The questions will be aimed at evaluating your understanding of the spoken language and cultural knowledge. Most questions will be quite similar to those used in Section 2 – Reading with Cultural Knowledge, and will include not only those that test your comprehension of the selection but also linguistic aspects (meaning of words and expressions, differences among countries), text structure and format (ideas presented in order of importance, in chronological order, etc.), and type (narration, description, debate). Additionally, however, there will be questions that apply only to spoken language such as:
-   Does the speaker sound friendly, aggressive?
-   Is the speaker a child, a teenager, a grown up, an old person?
-   Is the speaker in a hurry, bored?
-   Does the speaker sound comfortable, tired?

Remember that spoken language is not perfect: you are trying to express yourself on the fly and you cannot go back to fix the errors. When talking, even the most educated person makes minor mistakes, uses incomplete sentences and leaves ideas dangling.

To practice for this part of the test, ask different native Spanish speakers you may know to engage in conversations of various types, to make a presentation or to read a text of their choice. Listen carefully and try to pick up the differences in accents, expressions, and word selection. You can also listen to the radio or watch TV shows and news in Spanish. Switch channels to expose yourself to different countries. Watch a Mexican soap opera, a Colombian beauty pageant, Argentinean news, the Puerto Rican weather forecast. Again, pay attention to how they speak, the terms they use, their idioms, and, after listening for a while, try to answer the type of questions mentioned above.

Section 2 – Reading with Cultural Knowledge

Text #1

Enclavado en el mismo centro viejo de Madrid, lleno de voces, colores y aromas, El Rastro es un típico mercado al aire libre ubicado en el pintoresco y sonoro antiguo barrio judío de Lavapiés. Comenzó como un zoco tradicional de venta de artículos de segunda mano alrededor de 1740, y creció y se diversificó a través de los años hasta alcanzar hoy en día 3500 puestos.

La variedad de objetos ofrecidos es impresionante. Se pueden encontrar todo tipo de antigüedades (muebles de estilo, candiles antiguos, cuadros de tiempos pasados) en diversas condiciones de mantenimiento. Algunos de los objetos están tan bien conservados que parecen recién hechos. Otros se ven tan viejos y polvorientos que uno se pregunta quién puede tener interés en comprar un trasto en tan mal estado. Otro rubro muy bien representado es el de ropa y accesorios personales. Abundan pendientes, botones, colgantes, carteras, zapatos, gorras y sombreros, chales y chaquetas de toda época. Pero no todo es antiguo. Hay también puestos de artículos electrónicos de segunda mano, desguace de automóviles, y artesanías locales modernas. Si te decides a comprar algo, siguiendo la mejor tradición moruna de este tipo de mercado, el regateo es de rigor. El precio inicial es sólo el punto de partida para una serie de tira y afloja hasta llegar al acuerdo final.

Funciona los domingos y feriados desde la mañana y hasta después del almuerzo, y su fama es tal que no hay guía turística de Madrid que no lo incluya. Los locales acostumbran visitarlo también regularmente. Prefieren hacerlo los domingos temprano cuando hay más para ver y disfrutar, ya que alrededor de las dos de la tarde muchos de los puestos comienzan ya a recoger sus mercancías, y la gente y el bullicio dan lugar a un paisaje un poco desolado. Las reglamentaciones municipales no permiten puestos de alimentos y de animales vivos pero es muy fácil hacer un alto en el paseo y encontrar en el área dónde gustar los típicos barquillos madrileños o reparar a una auténtica tasca para tomar un aperitivo con tapas con los amigos luego de una mañana de exploración y vuelta al pasado.

Responder a las preguntas siguientes basándose en el texto anterior.

1. Un "zoco" es:
   a. Mercado de pulgas judío
   b. Mercado de pequeñas comunidades madrileñas
   c. Bazar tradicional de los países árabes
   d. Mercado de artesanos nativos

2. El texto indica que El Rastro fue creado:
   a. En el siglo XVII
   b. Por los moros
   c. En el siglo XVIII
   d. Por los judíos españoles

3. De acuerdo al texto, en El Rastro se pueden comprar, entre otras cosas:
   a. Antigüedades y objetos de época
   b. Comidas y bebidas
   c. Productos artesanales importados
   d. Todo lo anterior

4. El Rastro está abierto:
   a. Todas la mañanas
   b. Todos los domingos y días festivos
   c. Todos los domingos y días festivos a la mañana
   d. Los días feriados desde la mañana y hasta media tarde

5. El texto señala el uso del regateo en El Rastro. ¿Qué entiende usted por esto?
   a. La reducción del precio de un artículo
   b. La confirmación del precio de un artículo
   c. La negociación del precio de un artículo
   d. El cambio de unidad monetaria del precio de un artículo

6. Los "locales" mencionados en la segunda oración del último párrafo se refieren a:
   a. Los artesanos de la zona que venden sus productos en El Rastro
   b. Los madrileños que visitan El Rastro
   c. Las costumbres de los madrileños
   d. Los barquillos y otras comidas típicas

Text #2

Violeta Parra nació en 1917 en un pequeño pueblo en un área rural a unos 300 km al sur de Santiago en una prolífica familia de poetas, folcloristas y artistas. Pasó su infancia en el campo y, adolescente, se mudó a Santiago para vivir con su hermano y retomar sus estudios después de la muerte de su padre. No estando interesada en estudiar sino en el canto, abandonó la escuela y empezó a cantar con su hermana en pequeños bares, lugares de recreo y salones de barrio. Se casó con un empleado ferroviario y tuvo dos hijos, pero su primer matrimonio no duró demasiado debido a la vida inquieta y poco convencional de Violeta. Al principio de los años 50, impulsada por su amor al canto y al folclore, comenzó a recopilar tradiciones musicales a lo largo del país, las que resultaron en su libro *Cantos Folclóricos Chilenos* y en sus primeros discos. Viajó a Europa y a la Unión Soviética, y aprovechó estos viajes para grabar en Paris. De vuelta en Chile, fundó el Museo Nacional de Arte Folclórico en la ciudad de Concepción. Siguió cantando y grabando, y vivió durante un tiempo en Argentina con dos de sus hijos. Continuó viajando por Europa y expuso obras en el Louvre.

Aun cuando su obra incluye numerosos trabajos de calidad como artista plástica (pinturas, esculturas, cerámicas, bordados), Violeta Parra es mundialmente conocida por sus canciones. Su canción más famosa, *Gracias a la Vida*, fue popularizada en Latinoamérica por Mercedes Sosas y Alberto Cortez, y en Los Estados Unidos por Joan Baez. En la canción, himno folclórico celebrando la vida, Parra utiliza un lirismo romántico para agradecer a ésta la vista y el oído que le permiten apreciar lo que hay a su alrededor, y la voz, el corazón, la risa y el llanto que le permiten expresar sus sentimientos. Lamentablemente, un año después de componer *Gracias a la Vida*, y según algunos debido a desengaños amorosos, Parra se quitó la vida de un tiro en la cabeza. No alcanzó a cumplir los 50 años. Se ha dicho que en realidad, la intención de Parra al escribir la canción fue como nota de despedida, señalando, irónicamente, que buena salud, oportunidades y éxitos personales a nivel mundial no son suficientes para sobrellevar el dolor de la condición humana.

Responder a las preguntas siguientes basándose en el texto anterior.

1. Violeta Parra nació en
   a. Argentina
   b. Chile
   c. Perú
   d. Uruguay

2. Se puede inferir del texto que Violeta Parra:
   a. Nunca estuvo casada
   b. Estuvo casada una vez
   c. Estuvo casada dos veces
   d. Estuvo casada más de una vez

3. De acuerdo al texto, en su canción más famosa, Violeta Parra agradece:
   a. Estar viva
   b. Poder expresar sus sentimientos
   c. Los cinco sentidos
   d. El ser amado

4. Violeta Parra murió:
   a. De pena, después de un desengaño amoroso
   b. A consecuencia de un accidente con un arma de fuego
   c. Se suicidó
   d. Como resultado de una tumor en la cabeza

5. Lirismo se refiere a:
   a. Unión inefable del alma con Dios
   b. Ideal fundamental de equilibrio y sobriedad y de fidelidad a la naturaleza
   c. Imitación de modelos de la antigüedad
   d. Subjetividad en la expresión musical

6. Las ideas del primer párrafo están organizadas:
   a. En orden de importancia creciente
   b. En orden de importancia decreciente
   c. En orden temporal
   d. No tienen ningún orden particular

Text #3

El petróleo es un material orgánico generado por la descomposición de microorganismos provenientes de la tierra, el mar o lagos y que han sido enterrados bajo pesadas capas de sedimentos y cocinados a altas temperaturas durante miles de años. Está compuesto por largas cadenas de hidrógeno y carbono y pequeñas cantidades de nitrógeno, oxígeno y azufre. Una vez generado en la roca madre, rica en microorganismos, el petróleo migra hacia una zona permeable donde, atrapado por capas selladoras impermeables, es almacenado en los poros del reservorio. Si los organismos son sometidos a mayores temperaturas, las cadenas se rompen y, dados la temperatura y el tiempo necesarios, se transforma en gas, el cual está formado por los mismos elementos básicos que el petróleo pero en arreglos de cadenas mucho más cortas. Aunque originalmente formado a grandes profundidades bajo la corteza terrestre, los movimientos de ésta, tales como terremotos, levantamientos y desplazamientos, hacen que se pueda encontrar más cerca de la superficie.

Utilizando pruebas sísmicas, los geólogos estudian la distribución y tipos de rocas debajo de la superficie para localizar probables zonas donde el petróleo puede haberse depositado. Para extraerlo, se perfora un pozo en la tierra hasta llegar al reservorio. El pozo es bastante ancho en la superficie (de hasta 36 pulgadas) pero su diámetro disminuye a medida que se alcanzan profundidades mayores, llegando a ser a veces de sólo 7 pulgadas. Durante la perforación se circula dentro del pozo una mezcla de fluidos, sólidos y productos químicos llamado lodo de perforación. Este lodo está especialmente formulado para cada pozo para enfriar la broca, traer los cortes de roca a la superficie y mantener la presión adecuada. El pozo es entubado con cañerías para, entre otras cosas, prevenir desmoronamientos de las paredes del pozo dentro del mismo, evitar que agua, petróleo y gas almacenados en las formaciones rocosas entre en el pozo, y aislar las distintas capas de rocas unas de otras.

Durante y una vez terminada la perforación, se bajan herramientas de ensayo dentro del pozo para correr pruebas y establecer si hay petróleo y a qué profundidad. En caso de encontrarse una capa productiva, se baja una herramienta especial que contienen explosivos para perforar la cañería a la profundidad deseada y deja entrar el petróleo al pozo.

Responder a las preguntas siguientes basándose en el texto anterior

1. El petróleo está formado por:
   a. organismos terrestres
   b. organismos marinos
   c. organismos lacustres
   d. todos los anteriores

2. El petróleo se acumula en:
   a. la roca madre
   b. las capas selladoras
   c. la superficie de la tierra
   d. el reservorio

3. Para obtener gas hace falta:
   a. mayor temperatura y más tiempo que para obtener petróleo
   b. mayor temperatura y menos tiempo que para obtener petróleo
   c. menor temperatura y más tiempo que para obtener petróleo
   d. menor temperatura y menos tiempo que para obtener petróleo

4. Los estudios sísmicos
   a. indican con exactitud dónde hay petróleo
   b. producen terremotos
   c. ayudan a determinar las características de las rocas subterráneas
   d. son realizados dentro del pozo

5. La función del lodo de perforación es:
   a. enfriar la broca
   b. evitar el desmoronamiento del pozo
   c. aislar las diferentes capas rocosas unas de otras
   d. profundizar el pozo

6. El texto es:
   a. una narración
   b. un descripción
   c. una debate
   d. un análisis de causa y efecto

Text #4

La lufa es el fruto de una planta enredadera tropical que se puede encontrar en forma salvaje en la selva amazónica.   Es originaria de la India y fue introducida en Ecuador desde Colombia. Se parece a una calabaza, con un interior en forma de tubo hecho de fibras cortas naturalmente tejidas, y sus propiedades para el cuidado y exfoliación de la piel y para la activación de la circulación han sido reconocidas. Hoy en día es cultivada por unas 500 familias de agricultores en el valle de Manduriacos y comercializada por la cooperativa local Taller de la Lufa.

Una vez que se han recogido los frutos, éstos se ponen en remojo para poder quitar más fácilmente la cáscara gruesa que los recubre. Se eliminan también las semillas y se ponen a secar los frutos al sol. Una vez finalizado este lavado y secado, están listos para ser llevados a lomo de mula hasta el Taller. El Taller de la Lufa arregla un precio justo con los campesinos locales para la compra de la cosecha y provee el material para que los artesanos la combinen con algodón crudo, hilo de abacá, fibra de plátano y madera de balsa, entre otros materiales, para fabricar todo tipo de artículos para el baño, entre ellos esponjas, zapatillas y cepillos. También, después de un segundo lavado y de un planchado con rodillos metálicos, y usando tinturas de colores vivos se la usa para hacer cortinas, alfombras y adornos.

La mayor parte de los productos son exportados. Los principales compradores son los Estados Unidos y el Japón, pero ciertas líneas han tenido un gran éxito en España y Francia. De a poco, la penetración en el mercado nacional va incrementando. El Taller no sólo compra la cosecha de los agricultores y vende los productos fabricados por los artesanos, sino también asesora a ambos sobre calidad, precio y comercialización de sus productos.

Parte de las ganancias del Taller se reinvierten en el mismo, para mejorar sus instalaciones y equipos. Otra parte se utiliza para obras de ayuda social de los pueblos u obras de interés general. Con estos fondos se ha comprado un camión para ayudar a la gente a vender su producción en lugares más alejados donde pueden conseguir mejor precio por su producto. También se han reparado puentes y otras estructuras locales. En este momento el Taller tiene planeado construir una planta de secado de cacahuetes, desarrollar una empresa de turismo responsable, y construir un centro residencial-educativo.

Responder a las preguntas siguientes basándose en el texto anterior

1. La lufa se encuentra en forma salvaje en la selva amazónica significa que ésta crece:
    a. De forma desenfrenada
    b. De forma ilimitada
    c. De forma silvestre
    d. De forma irresponsable

2. Las esponjas de lufa son buenas para:
    a. Perder peso
    b. Eliminar las arrugas
    c. Remojarse la piel
    d. Quitar células muertas

3. El proceso de preparación de la lufa para la fabricación de artículos de baño es:
    a. Lavado
    b. Lavado y secado
    c. Lavado, secado y planchado
    d. Lavado, planchado y secado

4. El Taller de la Lufa es:
    a. Una compañía privada
    b. Una empresa pública
    c. Una entidad del estado
    d. Una cooperativa local

5. Los agricultores llevan sus productos a otros lugares alejados porque:
    a. El Taller de la Lufa no les compra la cosecha
    b. El Taller de la Lufa paga muy poco
    c. Otros compradores pagan más
    d. No se llevan bien con el Taller d la Lufa

6. El centro residencial-educativo planeado por el Taller de la Lufa es:
    a. Un complejo donde los estudiantes residen y estudian
    b. Una escuela ubicada en un barrio residencial
    c. Un centro para la educación de los habitantes de un barrio residencial
    d. Sólo para los estudiantes que no residen en la escuela

Text #5

Con el título de "El Renacimiento del Fresco en México", publicó en Le Cahier, famoso mensual de Parias, el año pasado, un interesante artículo el inteligente crítico y musicógrafo cubano Alejo Carpentier.

Da ocasión ese artículo para efectuar serias meditaciones sobre la vigorosa personalidad de Diego de Rivera, quien ha conquistado primero un renombre universal y comienza a tener popularidad en su adorado México.

Discutir la personalidad de Diego de Rivera, es ahora materia de varios volúmenes, así de proteica, complicada, variable y grandiosa. Alejo Carpentier, ha logrado, no obstante, efectuar una síntesis de todas las calidades de Diego en unas cuantas líneas; ellas revelan, al punto, la magnitud de este artista nuevo.

Diego es el poeta de la fuerza, de la grandiosidad social, del hecho conscientemente mexicanos; sus frescos, están hechos por un hombre, lleno de potencia creadora. Se ve en ellos la intención humana, cosmológica, social; se siente al contemplarlos el misterio de una aurora que brilla como algo nuevo en el alma.

El renacimiento del fresco en México es una realidad que tiene como principalísimo responsable a Diego aunque en esta hora hay otros pintores de murales con calidades tan valiosas como las que se encuentran en Diego; pero está fuera de discusión que sin el arrojo, la perseverancia, el gesto bélico y otras circunstanciás extraestéticas de Rivera, ese renacimiento no hubiera sido posible en esta época.

Pendiente de terminación la obra de colosales dimensiones que ha emprendido Diego en el Palacio Nacional, se ha dedicado en los últimos meses a pintar las paredes del Palacio de Gobierno del Estado de Morelos en la pintoresca Ciudad de Cuernavaca.

Esta obra, es un obsequio del Embajador de los E.U.A., en la república Mexicana a la Nación, pues por se cuenta la ejecuta Diego. Mr. Morrow ha sido uno de sus más adictos admiradores.

[....]

Se sigue notando en Diego el gusto por las actitudes combativas, caricaturescas, ridiculizantes, terriblemente irónicas. Esa cabeza de Hernán Cortés, visible en estas reproducciones, dice más sobre la ideología universal de Diego que todos sus discursos y declaraciones.
Desgraciadamente, esta preocupación ideológica hace desmerecer la obra de Diego en su calidad estética, hace a uno pensar, aun sin quererlo, en monstruosas ilustraciones de libros o en escenografía teatral.

Responder a las preguntas siguientes basándose en el texto anterior

1. Alejo Carpentier publicó un artículo sobre el renacimiento de los frescos en Méjico en:
    a. Méjico
    b. Cuba
    c. Francia
    d. Los Estados Unidos

2. De acuerdo al texto, la personalidad de Diego de Rivera es:
    a. Débil
    b. Simple
    c. Estable
    d. Ninguna de las anteriores

3. Diego de Rivera es responsable del renacimiento en Méjico:
    a. De las artes plásticas
    b. Del muralismo
    c. De las actitudes ridiculizantes
    d. De la pintura social

4. En el momento en que se escribió este texto, Diego de Rivera estaba trabajando en un fresco
    a. En la ciudad de Cuernavaca
    b. En el palacio de Gobierno de Morelos
    c. Pagado por un extranjero
    d. Todas las anteriores

5. A Diego de Rivera le gustan las imágenes:
    a. Serias
    b. Burlonas
    c. Plácidas
    d. De cabezas grandes

6. El artículo considera los frescos de Diego de Rivera:
   a. Importantes para Méjico
   b. Grandes pero poco significativos
   c. De poca monta
   d. Coloridos y simpáticos

Text #6

Hoy en día, más y más mujeres están cargo de su vida financiera. Algunas lo han hecho desde siempre. Otras se han visto obligadas a hacerlo debido a situaciones de la vida tales como no casarse, divorcio, muerte o incapacidad del esposo. Otras van de a poco tomando más responsabilidades, compartiendo decisiones. Aun cuando a veces lo ven como una tarea extra que se agrega a la larga lista de cosas por hacer, en el fondo están orgullosas de ponerse a la par de los hombres en una actividad de la que se han visto relegadas en muchísimas ocasiones.

Si bien algunas no están interesadas, la falta de participación no es buena. La mujer debe estar informada acerca de sus asuntos financieros. ¿Cuánto dinero entra en la casa mensualmente? ¿Cuánto hace falta para pagar las cuentas todos los meses? ¿Tiene deudas? ¿Cuánto puede ahorrar? ¿Tiene dinero invertido? Éstas son algunas preguntas básicas que toda mujer debe saber responder.

Un mayor conocimiento de la situación la hará sentirse más confiada y proclive a profundizar más en el asunto. El próximo paso sería definir sus objetivos financieros. ¿Qué quiere hacer? ¿Eliminar las deudas? ¿Ahorrar para pagar la educación de los hijos? ¿Tener lo suficiente como para vivir cómodamente una vez que se retire? La mujer tiene que estar informada y es mejor que tome parte en estas decisiones.

Una vez que ha decidido lo que se quiere, hay que decidir cómo lograrlo. Normalmente, ésta es la parte que más intimida ya que la cantidad y variedad de opciones es apabullante. Tarjetas de crédito y de débito, cuentas corrientes, cuentas de ahorro, depósitos a plazo fijo, cuentas de inversión, acciones, fondos, bonos, anualidades. Cada banco e institución financiera ofrece su propio menú. ¿Cómo manejarse con tantas cosas diferentes? Es aquí donde la ayuda de un profesional financiero hace la diferencia. Un consultor financiero ha estudiado profundamente todos estos aspectos y tiene a su alcance las herramientas apropiadas para realizar una evaluación realística de la situación y de los objetivos. Una vez realizado el análisis, el consultor puede ofrecerle los vehículos adecuados para alcanzar lo que desea.

Gómez, Gónzalez y Rodriguez es una firma especializada en análisis financieros. Sus consultores han sido capacitados para estudiar detalladamente su situación y objetivos financieros a corto y largo plazo. Todos los consultores tienen amplio conocimiento de lo que el mercado financiero ofrece, y no se detienen hasta encontrar las mejores opciones para usted y su familia. Su futuro y seguridad financieros están a su alcance.

No espere más; llámenos por teléfono o pase por nuestras oficinas donde siempre encontrará un consultor a su disposición.

Responder a las preguntas siguientes basándose en el texto anterior

1. Algunas de las mujeres ven las responsabilidades financieras como:
   a. Una carga extra
   b. Un deber
   c. Un derecho
   d. Una opción

2. Las mujeres que están a cargo de sus finanzas lo hacen porque:
   a. No tienen permitido contratar a un consultor que las ayude
   b. Es importante tener conocimiento y control de su propia vida financiera
   c. Una nueva ley las obliga a hacerlo
   d. No tienen nada mejor que hacer

3. De acuerdo al texto, una de las cuestiones básicas que toda mujer debería saber es:
   a. Cómo ahorrar
   b. Para qué ahorrar
   c. Cuánto ahorrar
   d. Por qué ahorrar

4. la cantidad y variedad de opciones financieras son:
   a. Muy limitadas
   b. Sólo conocidas por los consultores
   c. Abrumadoras
   d. Fuera del alcance de las mujeres

5. Los consultores financieros pueden:
   a. Ayudar a invertir el dinero
   b. Analizar los objetivos financieros
   c. Evaluar la situación financiera
   d. Todo lo anterior

6. El texto:
   a. Informa a las mujeres de sus derechos financieros
   b. Dice que las mujeres son financieramente incapaces
   c. Es un aviso de una consultoría financiera
   d. Recluta mujeres para trabajar en firmas financieras

Visual #1

¿Cuál de las opciones siguientes describe de mejor manera esta pintura de Emanuel Leutze de 1843?

    a. Fernando de Magallanes presentando a los reyes de España los primeros nativos traídos de América.

    b. Galileo Galilei retractándose de su teoría de que la Tierra gira alrededor del Sol ante los Reyes Católicos.

    c. Hernán Cortés explicando a la reina Sofía y al rey Juan Carlos de España por qué no pudo traer oro y plata del nuevo continente.

    d. Cristóbal Colón solicitando a Isabel de Castilla y a Fernando de Aragón fondos para financiar su viaje a las Indias.

La foto anterior, tomada en 1912 por la expedición de Bingham, muestra las ruinas de:
   a. Machu Pichu, la ciudad perdida de los incas, construida en Perú en el siglo XV.
   b. Teotihuacán, un templo construido por los mayas en el siglo XVII en Colombia.
   c. Un templo construido por los indios patagones en Bolivia.
   d. Un templo construido por los conquistadores españoles para los dioses aztecas en el siglo XII.

Visual #3

La pintura *La Posta de San Luis* de Juan León Pallière reproducida aquí representa:
  a. Gauchos comiendo después de una jineteada
  b. Viajeros alimentándose en un alto en el camino
  c. Jinetes recuperándose después de la doma de caballos
  d. Campesinos descansando después del arreo de ganado

Section 3: Writing

Essay

Escriba un texto de por lo menos 120 palabras sobre el siguiente tema.

Durante muchos años, el petróleo y el carbón han sido los combustibles principales utilizados para la generación de energía eléctrica. En la última década, el gas ha ido reclamando su parte del mercado. Aun cuando la tecnología geotérmica y la de mareas no son todavía económicamente viables, otras fuentes de energía renovables tales como viento y sol han ido incrementando poco a poco su importancia como generadoras de electricidad. ¿Le parece que estas fuentes de energía renovables tienen un futuro en los Estados Unidos y en el mundo como generadoras principales de energía eléctrica?

Interpersonal Writing: Response to an email, memo or letter.

Responda a la carta siguiente, declinando la invitación, explicando por qué y sugiriendo una solución.

Bogotá, 12 de enero de 2014

Estimado Dr. López Urrutia:

Del 19 al 23 de agosto de 2014 tendrá lugar en la ciudad de Bogotá el Segundo Congreso Colombiano de Conservación de Recursos Naturales, el foro nacional más importante para todo lo concerniente a la conservación de los recursos naturales, la fauna y la flora. Visto sus conocimientos y trabajos relacionados con los efectos en los cetáceos de las actividades de exploración y explotación petroleras costa afuera de Colombia, deseamos invitarlo a participar como moderador del panel de discusión abierta "Impactos de las actividades de prospección sísmica en la fauna marina de Colombia". El panel se llevará a cabo el 21 de agosto a las 9 de la mañana y durará aproximadamente una hora. Tentativamente, los panelistas serán el Dr. Carlos Alberto Gutiérrez, la Dra. María de los Ángeles Valdeverde y el Licenciado Augusto Pérez Roldán. Agradeceríamos confirmación de su participación a la brevedad. Esperando contar con su presencia, lo saluda muy cordialmente Alberto Gómez Cabrera Coordinador General Asociación Colombiana de Conservación de Recursos Naturales

Interpersonal Writing: Writing task based on a given text

Hoy se le comunicó oficialmente de parte de la Comisión de Amigos del Arte, al pintor David Alfaro Siqueiros, que se le prohibía dar su tercera conferencia sobre arte mejicano. Esta decisión no es más que un resultado de la mojigatería. La citada decisión que cubre de ridículo a la institución arriba mencionada comprueba más que nada que la situación de ciertos problemas no pueden ser encarados sin que los que debieran estar interesados en el asunto decidan eludirlos. Siqueiros ha venido a demostrar a los artistas nuestros la forma en que se realizó el movimiento pictórico más interesante del momento actual. Y ahora se le prohíbe que siga en su ciclo de disertaciones.

[...]

"En esas dos primeras conferencias no yo no hice más que relatar los hechos históricos concretos de los movimientos de pintura monumental en que he participado. Es evidente que esos dos movimientos, considerados como los de mayor trascendencia de la época actual por los más importantes críticos europeos, no se produjeron de manera accidental, sino que responden a realidades sociales fundamentales. Ocultar esas realidades fundamentales, las causas sociales que las impulsaron, los fenómenos políticos que le dieron vida, hubiera sido cometer una innobleza frente a los deseos de la masa intelectual argentina, que anhelaba como tal del mismo, dando, en cambio, solamente una relación cronológica, superficial y, sin sentido alguno. Igual cosa habría acontecido si en el caso del bloque de pintores murales de Los Ángeles me hubiera limitado a hablar de los nombres y de las dimensiones de las obras monumentales realizadas.

Lo que vale fundamentalmente en el movimiento de pintores de Los Ángeles, es precisamente su carácter social. El hecho de que su naturaleza constituye la continuación superada del renacimiento mejicano, en que rectifica los errores del primero, encuentra una técnica correspondiente y toma resueltamente el camino de la ideología revolucionaria y del método dialéctico que corresponde a esa ideología. No decir nada sobre este método dialéctico, por razones de suspicacia política, sería ocultar lo más importante del movimiento plástico contemporáneo que radica precisamente en el uso de un método científico para la producción plástica moderna."

Basándose en el texto anterior, escriba un texto breve de por lo menos 120 palabras defendiendo la siguiente afirmación.

La mayoría de los movimientos artísticos modernos tienen origen en los impulsos revolucionarios de las masas, y su valor radica en haber buscado la expresión plástica que expresa los anhelos de los pueblos y su íntima relación con la vida.

Section 4 – Speaking

The Speaking portion of the test has three parts: two involving presentational skills and one involving interpersonal speaking

In the first presentational task you will be required to discuss a topic related to a passage you have already read in the Writing section. You will have half a minute to read the instructions and one minute to re-read the text. For example:
- Based on the text about El Rastro in Section 2, explain why and what you like and dislike about that kind of market.
- Cooperatives tend to help smaller agricultural communities, especially in less developed areas or in those with a big indigenous population that has fewer resources. Do you think the same model can be applied to other products besides those of the land? Use the text about El Taller de la Lufa in Section 2 as a reference.
- Based on the text on Section 3, do you think that art should not be linked to politics?

In the second presentational task, you will be asked to express your opinion or make a 2-minute presentation about a given topic. You will listen to the topic and, after a pause, to the question. You can practice using a variety of topics such as:
- Some said that James Bond movies are getting harder to follow at times and inconsistent with things that happened in previous ones. *Question*: Do you think this is a problem just with James Bond movies or that it also appears in other series of movies?
- Many Latin-American countries have been developing eco-tourism. They believe it is a good way to increase the influx of hard currency without damaging their environment. *Question*: Do you think eco-tourism really preserves natural resources?
- Smart phones give us the flexibility to communicate with others regardless of where we are. This flexibility also entails being expected to respond from anywhere. Some consider that, whether

related to work or of personal character, this expectation of availability at all times is an invasion to our private life. *Question*: Do you feel you have been pushed to respond to others at their convenience and not yours?

The interpersonal speaking part of the test will consist of your participation in a simulated conversation. You will be given an outline of the conversation but not the actual words the other person will use. It may be a conversation between friends, with a colleague, or an interview, for example. Some scenarios you can use to practice with a partner could be:

-   You talk with your mother to organize a surprise party for your younger brother.
-   You talk with a colleague to set up a meeting to discuss sales goals for the following month.
-   A lady stops you in the street and asks you the best way to get to the Museum of Fine Arts.
-   You are interviewed for a position as second grade Spanish teacher.

For all three speaking tasks, you will have some time to prepare your answers. Read the instructions carefully. Organize your ideas. You can present them in order of importance, in chronological order or in cause and effect order. Stay true to the topic and question. Say as much as you can, but speak clearly and do not rush.

Answers and Explanation

Answers for Text #1

1. C: A "zoco" is a traditional market from the Arab countries of North Africa, brought to Spain by the Moors. The end of the second paragraph mentions the Moors and the traditional customs of these markets. Answer (a) is incorrect because El Rastro is located in an old Jewish neighborhood but is not a traditional Jewish flea market. Answer (b) is incorrect because it is never mentioned in the text that those selling at the market are from small communities from Madrid. Answer (d) is incorrect because the text mentions local craftsmen selling their products at the market live in the area but are not necessarily from it.

2. C: The first paragraph states that El Rastro was created in 1740, a year that belongs to the 18th century. Answer (a) is incorrect because the 17th century refers to the 1600s. The text never mentions who created El Rastro, therefore answers (b) and (d) are incorrect.

3. A: The second paragraph mentions antique items and objects. Answer (b) is incorrect because the last paragraph states that municipal regulations forbid the sale of food. Answer (c) is incorrect because the text does not mention imported crafts; the second paragraph mentions local crafts. Since answers (b) and (c) are incorrect, answer (d) is incorrect.

4. B: The last paragraph states that El Rastro is open Sundays and holidays in the morning until after lunch. Answer (a) is incorrect because it implies every morning, weekdays, weekends and holidays included. Answer (c) is incorrect because it indicates it is open Sundays and holidays only in the mornings. Answer (d) is incorrect because it suggests it is open only on holidays.

5. C: The meaning of "regatear" is to haggle or to barter, and refers to the negotiation of the price of an item and usually takes place in this kind of market. Answer (a) is incorrect because a reduction of the price may be a consequence of haggling but it is not the act itself. Answer (b) is incorrect because confirmation of the price may be a consequence of haggling but it is not the act itself. Answer (d) is incorrect because currency exchange may be part of haggling but it is not the act itself.

6. B: The second sentence of the last paragraph refers to the local people from Madrid that visits the market. Answer (a) is incorrect because the last paragraph talks about those visiting El Rastro, and not about those selling their products at the market. Answer (c) is incorrect because in the sentence the subject is the people who are used to do something and not the habit itself. Answer (d) is incorrect because food items cannot visit a market.

Answers for Text #2

1. B: The first sentence states Parra was born in a town south of Santiago, the capital of Chile. Since Santiago is in Chile, answers (a), (c) and (d) are incorrect.

2. D: In the middle of the first paragraph, it is stated that "her first marriage did not last long". Therefore she was married at least twice, making answers (a) and (b) incorrect. The

text does not make any other reference to her marriages, consequently we do not know if she was married two or more times.

3. B: According to the text, in her song, Parra is thankful for her voice, her heart, laughing and crying, which allow her to express her feelings. Answer (a) is incorrect because the text does not mention being alive as one of the things Parra is thankful. Answer (c) is incorrect because just two senses (sight and hearing) are mentioned. Answer (d) is incorrect because the text does not mention the love one as one of the things Parra is thankful.

4. C: Parra committed suicide taking her own life with a gunshot to her head. Answer (a) is incorrect because she did not die of a broken heart. Answer (b) is incorrect because the gunshot was not an accident. Answer (d) is incorrect because she did not have any tumor in her head.

5. D: Subjectivity in literary and musical expression is the definition of lyricism. Answer (a) is incorrect as the union of the soul with God is part of the definition of mysticism. Answers (b) and (c) are incorrect because they belong to the definition of classicism.

6. C: in the first paragraph, facts are presented chronologically. Answers (a) and (b) are incorrect because the ideas of the first paragraph are not in order of importance. Answer (d) is incorrect because the ideas of the first paragraph have a certain order.

Answers for Text #3

1. D: The first sentence of the text says oil is formed from terrestrial, marine, and lacustrine microorganisms.

2. D: The text states oil is stored in the pores of the reservoir. Answer (a) is incorrect because the source rock is where the oil is generated. Answer (b) is incorrect because the sealing layers are impermeable therefore cannot store oil. Answer (c) is incorrect because oil is stored at different depths below the surface of the Earth.

3. A: Oil subjected to higher temperatures over time converts to gas. Answer (b) is incorrect because you need time to generate oil and then more time to convert it to gas. Answer (c) is incorrect because higher temperatures are needed to break the long hydrocarbon chains of oil into the short ones of gas. Answer (d) is incorrect because lower temperatures do not break the oil's long chains and time is needed to achieve this breakage.

4. C: Geologists use seismic to study the distribution and characteristics of the rocks under the surface. Answer (a) is incorrect because the text states seismic is used to find <u>probable</u> places where oil <u>may</u> exist. Answer (b) is incorrect because seismic studies do not produce earthquakes. Answer (d) is incorrect because seismic surveys are done to select where to drill a well therefore they are run before drilling a well and not inside it.

5. A: One of the functions of the drilling mud is to cool the drilling bit. Answer (b) is incorrect because it is a function of the casing to prevent the collapse of the walls of the well. Answer (c) is incorrect because it is a function of the casing to isolate the different rock layers from each other. Answer (d) is incorrect because the drilling bit is the element that deepens the well.

6. B: The text describes how oil is formed and brought to the surface. Answer (a) is incorrect because the text does not narrate a story. Answer (c) is incorrect because the text is not a discussion of pros and cons. Answer (d) is incorrect because the text does not analyze the causes and effects of an event.

Answers for Text #4

1. C: The first sentence states that the plant can be found growing on its own, not purposely cultivated. Answer (a) is incorrect because the text does not say the plant grows unrestrained. Answer (b) is incorrect because the text does not say the plant grows without limits. Answer (d) is incorrect because the text does not say the plant grows irresponsibly.

2. C: The loofah sponge is good for exfoliating the skin, a process that removes superficial dead cells. Answer (a) is incorrect because the text does not mention losing weight anywhere. Answer (b) is incorrect because the text does not say using a loofah sponge will eliminate wrinkles. Answer (d) is incorrect because the fruit of the loofah is soaked to remove its skin; a loofah sponge is not use to soak a person's skin.

3. B: To make bath products the loofah is first washed to remove the skin and seeds and then dried in the sun. Answer (a) is incorrect because the loofah is not only washed but also dried in the sun. Answer (c) is incorrect because the loofah is not ironed to make bath products; the text says it is ironed to make curtains, rugs and decorations. Answer (d) is incorrect for the same reasons answer c) is incorrect.

4. D: The first paragraph says that the Taller de la Lufa is a local cooperative. Answer (a) is incorrect; the Taller de la Lufa is not a private company. Answer (b) is incorrect; the Taller de la Lufa is not a public company. Answer (c) is incorrect; the Taller de la Lufa is not a state entity.

5. C: The farmers take their product to other places to get a better price. Answer (a) is incorrect because the Taller de la Lufa buys the farmers' crop. Answer (b) is incorrect because the Taller de la Lufa pays the farmers a just price. Answer (d) is incorrect because it does not say the farmers do not get along well with the Taller.

6. A: Students live and study at the center. Answer (b) is incorrect because the center is not a school in a residential neighborhood. Answer(c) is incorrect because the center is not a place to educate people who live in a residential neighborhood. Answer (d) is incorrect because the center is not just for students that do not live in it.

Answers for Text #5

1. C: The article was published in Le Cahier in Paris, France. Answer (a) is incorrect; the article is about a Mexican artistic development but was not published in Mexico. Answer (b) is incorrect, Carpentier was born in Cuba. Answer (d) is incorrect; the article mentions the USA ambassador but the article was not published in the USA.

2. D: According to the article, Rivera's personality was vigorous, complicated and variable. Answer (a) is incorrect; Rivera's personality was vigorous not weak. Answer (b) is incorrect; Rivera's personality was complicated not simple. Answer (c) is incorrect; Rivera's personality was variable not stable.

- 58 -

3. B: Rivera is considered to be responsible for the renaissance of the murals in Mexico. Answer (a) is incorrect; Rivera is responsible just for the renaissance of the murals in particular, not of all plastic art in general. Answer (c) is incorrect; Rivera just liked attitudes that ridicule. Answer (d) is incorrect; Rivera was not responsible for a renaissance of social painting.

4. D: Rivera was working on a fresco in the Palacio de Gobierno del Estado de Morelos in the city of Cuernavaca. The fresco was a gift of the American ambassador.

5. B: Rivera liked mocking images. Answer (a) is incorrect; Rivera liked caricatures and images that ridicule, not serious ones. Answer (c) is incorrect; Rivera liked aggressive, not placid attitudes. Answer (d) is incorrect; Rivera painted big heads but the text does not specifically say he liked them.

6. A: The text emphasizes the importance of Rivera's frescos in the renaissance of this type of art in Mexico. Answer (b) is incorrect; Rivera's frescos are big and the text considers them very important. Answer (c) is incorrect; the text considers Rivera's frescos very important. Answer (d) is incorrect; the text does not say Rivera's frescos are colorful and charming.

Answers for Text #6

1. A: The first paragraph says some women see the financial responsibilities as an extra added to their list of things to do. Answer (b) is incorrect; taking care of financial responsibilities is not an obligation. Answer (c) is incorrect; the text does not say that taking care of financial responsibilities is a right women have. Answer (d) is incorrect; the text does not say that taking care of financial responsibilities is an option women have.

2. B: The text states that women should know about and have control over their financial situation. Answer (a) is incorrect; women are allowed to hire a consultant to help them with their finances. Answer (c) is incorrect; there are no laws forcing women to take care of their finances. Answer (d) is incorrect; women do not take care of their finances because they do not have anything better to do.

3. C: The second paragraph includes how much to save as one of the basic question every woman should know how to answer. Answer (a) is incorrect; the text does not say how to save. Answer (b) is incorrect; the third paragraph includes a question about saving for kids' college but it is not one of the basic questions a woman should know how to answer. Answer (d) is incorrect; the text does not say why to save.

4. C: The amount and variety of financial options are overwhelming. Answer (a) is incorrect; quantity and variety are not very limited. Answer (b) is incorrect; financial options are not known only by consultants. Answer (d) is incorrect; women have access to financial options.

5. D: Financial consultants can help invest money, analyze financial objectives, _and_ assess financial situations.

6. C: The last two paragraphs clearly advertise the services of a financial firm. The first four paragraphs establish the basis for the advertisement. Answer (a) is incorrect; the text does

- 59 -

not inform women about their financial rights. Answer (b) is incorrect; the text does not say women are financially incapable; on the contrary, it encourages women to take care of their finances. Answer (d) is incorrect; the text is not trying to recruit women to work for financial firms.

Answer for Visual #1

A: Incorrect. Fernando de Magallanes died in the Philippine Islands and never returned to Spain from his circumnavigation of the Earth. The first natives brought from America were presented to the King of Spain by Cristóbal Colón. The painting does not show any natives.
B: Incorrect. Galileo Galilei defended his heliocentric theory in a book and was later tried by the Holy Office or Roman Inquisition and forced to recant.
C: Incorrect. Queen Sofía and King Juan Carlos are the current monarchs of Spain. Hernán Cortés died in 1547.
D: Correct. Cristóbal Colón asked Isabel and Fernando for financial support to find a route to the East Indies by sailing west.

Answer for Visual #2

A: Correct. The ruins are high in the mountains and have the typical terraces and regularly shaped buildings of the Incas.
B: Incorrect. Teotihuacán is a pre-Colombian city in Mexico.
C: Incorrect. The Patagones, included in the broader category of the Teheulches, was a group of natives that lived in the South of Argentina and never reached Bolivia.
D: Incorrect. The Spanish conquistadores never built any temples to be used to worship Native American gods.

Answer for Visual #3

A: Incorrect. The word "jineteada" means "rodeo". The picture does not show any horses. We cannot infer the characters in the picture have been training any.
B: Correct. The title of the painting indicates it depicts a stop on the road. A small building, the "posta" is seen in the background. There is also a stagecoach to its right.
C: Incorrect. As mentioned in answer a), the picture does not show any horses and we cannot infer the characters in the picture have been training any.
D: Incorrect. The picture does not show any cattle. We cannot infer the characters in the picture have been herding any.

Secret Key #1 - Time is Your Greatest Enemy

Pace Yourself

Wear a watch. At the beginning of the test, check the time (or start a chronometer on your watch to count the minutes), and check the time after every few questions to make sure you are "on schedule."

If you are forced to speed up, do it efficiently. Usually one or more answer choices can be eliminated without too much difficulty. Above all, don't panic. Don't speed up and just begin guessing at random choices. By pacing yourself, and continually monitoring your progress against your watch, you will always know exactly how far ahead or behind you are with your available time. If you find that you are one minute behind on the test, don't skip one question without spending any time on it, just to catch back up. Take 15 fewer seconds on the next four questions, and after four questions you'll have caught back up. Once you catch back up, you can continue working each problem at your normal pace.

Furthermore, don't dwell on the problems that you were rushed on. If a problem was taking up too much time and you made a hurried guess, it must be difficult. The difficult questions are the ones you are most likely to miss anyway, so it isn't a big loss. It is better to end with more time than you need than to run out of time.

Lastly, sometimes it is beneficial to slow down if you are constantly getting ahead of time. You are always more likely to catch a careless mistake by working more slowly than quickly, and among very high-scoring test takers (those who are likely to have lots of time left over), careless errors affect the score more than mastery of material.

Secret Key #2 - Guessing is not Guesswork

You probably know that guessing is a good idea. Unlike other standardized tests, there is no penalty for getting a wrong answer. Even if you have no idea about a question, you still have a 20-25% chance of getting it right.

Most test takers do not understand the impact that proper guessing can have on their score. Unless you score extremely high, guessing will significantly contribute to your final score.

Monkeys Take the Test

What most test takers don't realize is that to insure that 20-25% chance, you have to guess randomly. If you put 20 monkeys in a room to take this test, assuming they answered once per question and behaved themselves, on average they would get 20-25% of the questions correct. Put 20 test takers in the room, and the average will be much lower among guessed questions. Why?

1. The test writers intentionally write deceptive answer choices that "look" right. A test taker has no idea about a question, so he picks the "best looking" answer, which is often wrong. The monkey has no idea what looks good and what doesn't, so it will consistently be right about 20-25% of the time.
2. Test takers will eliminate answer choices from the guessing pool based on a hunch or intuition. Simple but correct answers often get excluded, leaving a 0% chance of being correct. The monkey has no clue, and often gets lucky with the best choice.

This is why the process of elimination endorsed by most test courses is flawed and detrimental to your performance. Test takers don't guess; they make an ignorant stab in the dark that is usually worse than random.

$5 Challenge

Let me introduce one of the most valuable ideas of this course—the $5 challenge:

You only mark your "best guess" if you are willing to bet $5 on it.
You only eliminate choices from guessing if you are willing to bet $5 on it.

Why $5? Five dollars is an amount of money that is small yet not insignificant, and can really add up fast (20 questions could cost you $100). Likewise, each answer choice on one question of the test will have a small impact on your overall score, but it can really add up to a lot of points in the end.

The process of elimination IS valuable. The following shows your chance of guessing it right:

If you eliminate wrong answer choices until only this many remain:	Chance of getting it correct:
1	100%
2	50%
3	33%

However, if you accidentally eliminate the right answer or go on a hunch for an incorrect answer, your chances drop dramatically—to 0%. By guessing among all the answer choices, you are GUARANTEED to have a shot at the right answer.

That's why the $5 test is so valuable. If you give up the advantage and safety of a pure guess, it had better be worth the risk.

What we still haven't covered is how to be sure that whatever guess you make is truly random. Here's the easiest way:

Always pick the first answer choice among those remaining.

Such a technique means that you have decided, **before you see a single test question**, exactly how you are going to guess, and since the order of choices tells you nothing about which one is correct, this guessing technique is perfectly random.

This section is not meant to scare you away from making educated guesses or eliminating choices; you just need to define when a choice is worth eliminating. The $5 test, along with a pre-defined random guessing strategy, is the best way to make sure you reap all of the benefits of guessing.

Secret Key #3 - Practice Smarter, Not Harder

Many test takers delay the test preparation process because they dread the awful amounts of practice time they think necessary to succeed on the test. We have refined an effective method that will take you only a fraction of the time.

There are a number of "obstacles" in the path to success. Among these are answering questions, finishing in time, and mastering test-taking strategies. All must be executed on the day of the test at peak performance, or your score will suffer. The test is a mental marathon that has a large impact on your future.

Just like a marathon runner, it is important to work your way up to the full challenge. So first you just worry about questions, and then time, and finally strategy:

Success Strategy

1. Find a good source for practice tests.
2. If you are willing to make a larger time investment, consider using more than one study guide. Often the different approaches of multiple authors will help you "get" difficult concepts.
3. Take a practice test with no time constraints, with all study helps, "open book." Take your time with questions and focus on applying strategies.
4. Take a practice test with time constraints, with all guides, "open book."
5. Take a final practice test without open material and with time limits.

If you have time to take more practice tests, just repeat step 5. By gradually exposing yourself to the full rigors of the test environment, you will condition your mind to the stress of test day and maximize your success.

Secret Key #4 - Prepare, Don't Procrastinate

Let me state an obvious fact: if you take the test three times, you will probably get three different scores. This is due to the way you feel on test day, the level of preparedness you have, and the version of the test you see. Despite the test writers' claims to the contrary, some versions of the test WILL be easier for you than others.

Since your future depends so much on your score, you should maximize your chances of success. In order to maximize the likelihood of success, you've got to prepare in advance. This means taking practice tests and spending time learning the information and test taking strategies you will need to succeed.

Never go take the actual test as a "practice" test, expecting that you can just take it again if you need to. Take all the practice tests you can on your own, but when you go to take the official test, be prepared, be focused, and do your best the first time!

Secret Key #5 - Test Yourself

Everyone knows that time is money. There is no need to spend too much of your time or too little of your time preparing for the test. You should only spend as much of your precious time preparing as is necessary for you to get the score you need.

Once you have taken a practice test under real conditions of time constraints, then you will know if you are ready for the test or not.

If you have scored extremely high the first time that you take the practice test, then there is not much point in spending countless hours studying. You are already there.

Benchmark your abilities by retaking practice tests and seeing how much you have improved. Once you consistently score high enough to guarantee success, then you are ready.

If you have scored well below where you need, then knuckle down and begin studying in earnest. Check your improvement regularly through the use of practice tests under real conditions. Above all, don't worry, panic, or give up. The key is perseverance!

Then, when you go to take the test, remain confident and remember how well you did on the practice tests. If you can score high enough on a practice test, then you can do the same on the real thing.

General Strategies

The most important thing you can do is to ignore your fears and jump into the test immediately. Do not be overwhelmed by any strange-sounding terms. You have to jump into the test like jumping into a pool—all at once is the easiest way.

Make Predictions

As you read and understand the question, try to guess what the answer will be. Remember that several of the answer choices are wrong, and once you begin reading them, your mind will immediately become cluttered with answer choices designed to throw you off. Your mind is typically the most focused immediately after you have read the question and digested its contents. If you can, try to predict what the correct answer will be. You may be surprised at what you can predict.

Quickly scan the choices and see if your prediction is in the listed answer choices. If it is, then you can be quite confident that you have the right answer. It still won't hurt to check the other answer choices, but most of the time, you've got it!

Answer the Question

It may seem obvious to only pick answer choices that answer the question, but the test writers can create some excellent answer choices that are wrong. Don't pick an answer just because it sounds right, or you believe it to be true. It MUST answer the question. Once you've made your selection, always go back and check it against the question and make sure that you didn't misread the question and that the answer choice does answer the question posed.

Benchmark

After you read the first answer choice, decide if you think it sounds correct or not. If it doesn't, move on to the next answer choice. If it does, mentally mark that answer choice. This doesn't mean that you've definitely selected it as your answer choice, it just means that it's the best you've seen thus far. Go ahead and read the next choice. If the next choice is worse than the one you've already selected, keep going to the next answer choice. If the next choice is better than the choice you've already selected, mentally mark the new answer choice as your best guess.

The first answer choice that you select becomes your standard. Every other answer choice must be benchmarked against that standard. That choice is correct until proven otherwise by another answer choice beating it out. Once you've decided that no other answer choice seems as good, do one final check to ensure that your answer choice answers the question posed.

Valid Information

Don't discount any of the information provided in the question. Every piece of information may be necessary to determine the correct answer. None of the information in the question is there to throw you off (while the answer choices will certainly have information to throw you off). If two seemingly unrelated topics are discussed, don't ignore either. You can be confident there is a relationship, or it wouldn't be included in the question, and you are probably going to have to determine what is that relationship to find the answer.

Avoid "Fact Traps"

Don't get distracted by a choice that is factually true. Your search is for the answer that answers the question. Stay focused and don't fall for an answer that is true but irrelevant. Always go back to the question and make sure you're choosing an answer that actually answers the question and is not just a true statement. An answer can be factually correct, but it MUST answer the question asked. Additionally, two answers can both be seemingly correct, so be sure to read all of the answer choices, and make sure that you get the one that BEST answers the question.

Milk the Question

Some of the questions may throw you completely off. They might deal with a subject you have not been exposed to, or one that you haven't reviewed in years. While your lack of knowledge about the subject will be a hindrance, the question itself can give you many clues that will help you find the correct answer. Read the question carefully and look for clues. Watch particularly for adjectives and nouns describing difficult terms or words that you don't recognize. Regardless of whether you completely understand a word or not, replacing it with a synonym, either provided or one you more familiar with, may help you to understand what the questions are asking. Rather than wracking your mind about specific detailed information concerning a difficult term or word, try to use mental substitutes that are easier to understand.

The Trap of Familiarity

Don't just choose a word because you recognize it. On difficult questions, you may not recognize a number of words in the answer choices. The test writers don't put "make-believe" words on the test, so don't think that just because you only recognize all the words in one answer choice that that answer choice must be correct. If you only recognize words in one answer choice, then focus on that one. Is it correct? Try your best to determine if it is correct. If it is, that's great. If not, eliminate it. Each word and answer choice you eliminate increases your chances of getting the question correct, even if you then have to guess among the unfamiliar choices.

Eliminate Answers

Eliminate choices as soon as you realize they are wrong. But be careful! Make sure you consider all of the possible answer choices. Just because one appears right, doesn't mean that the next one won't be even better! The test writers will usually put more than one good answer choice for every question, so read all of them. Don't worry if you are stuck between two that seem right. By getting down to just two remaining possible choices, your odds are now 50/50. Rather than wasting too much time, play the odds. You are guessing, but guessing wisely because you've been able to knock out some of the answer choices that you know are wrong. If you are eliminating choices and realize that the last answer choice you are left with is also obviously wrong, don't panic. Start over and consider each choice again. There may easily be something that you missed the first time and will realize on the second pass.

Tough Questions

If you are stumped on a problem or it appears too hard or too difficult, don't waste time. Move on! Remember though, if you can quickly check for obviously incorrect answer choices, your chances of guessing correctly are greatly improved. Before you completely give up, at least try to knock out a couple of possible answers. Eliminate what you can and then guess at the remaining answer choices before moving on.

Brainstorm

If you get stuck on a difficult question, spend a few seconds quickly brainstorming. Run through the complete list of possible answer choices. Look at each choice and ask yourself, "Could this answer the question satisfactorily?" Go through each answer choice and consider it independently of the others. By systematically going through all possibilities, you may find something that you would otherwise overlook. Remember though that when you get stuck, it's important to try to keep moving.

Read Carefully

Understand the problem. Read the question and answer choices carefully. Don't miss the question because you misread the terms. You have plenty of time to read each question thoroughly and make sure you understand what is being asked. Yet a happy medium must be attained, so don't waste too much time. You must read carefully, but efficiently.

Face Value

When in doubt, use common sense. Always accept the situation in the problem at face value. Don't read too much into it. These problems will not require you to make huge leaps of logic. The test writers aren't trying to throw you off with a cheap trick. If you have to go beyond creativity and make a leap of logic in order to have an answer choice answer the question, then you should look at the other answer choices. Don't overcomplicate the problem by creating theoretical relationships or explanations that will warp time or space. These are normal problems rooted in reality. It's just that the applicable relationship or explanation may not be readily apparent and you have to figure things out. Use your common sense to interpret anything that isn't clear.

Prefixes

If you're having trouble with a word in the question or answer choices, try dissecting it. Take advantage of every clue that the word might include. Prefixes and suffixes can be a huge help. Usually they allow you to determine a basic meaning. Pre- means before, post- means after, pro - is positive, de- is negative. From these prefixes and suffixes, you can get an idea of the general meaning of the word and try to put it into context. Beware though of any traps. Just because con- is the opposite of pro-, doesn't necessarily mean congress is the opposite of progress!

Hedge Phrases

Watch out for critical hedge phrases, led off with words such as "likely," "may," "can," "sometimes," "often," "almost," "mostly," "usually," "generally," "rarely," and "sometimes." Question writers insert these hedge phrases to cover every possibility. Often an answer choice will be wrong simply because it leaves no room for exception. Unless the situation calls for them, avoid answer choices that have definitive words like "exactly," and "always."

Switchback Words

Stay alert for "switchbacks." These are the words and phrases frequently used to alert you to shifts in thought. The most common switchback word is "but." Others include "although," "however," "nevertheless," "on the other hand," "even though," "while," "in spite of," "despite," and "regardless of."

New Information

Correct answer choices will rarely have completely new information included. Answer choices typically are straightforward reflections of the material asked about and will directly relate to the question. If a new piece of information is included in an answer choice that doesn't even seem to relate to the topic being asked about, then that answer choice is likely incorrect. All of the information needed to answer the question is usually provided for you in the question. You should not have to make guesses that are unsupported or choose answer choices that require unknown information that cannot be reasoned from what is given.

Time Management

On technical questions, don't get lost on the technical terms. Don't spend too much time on any one question. If you don't know what a term means, then odds are you aren't going to get much further since you don't have a dictionary. You should be able to immediately recognize whether or not you know a term. If you don't, work with the other clues that you have—the other answer choices and terms provided—but don't waste too much time trying to figure out a difficult term that you don't know.

Contextual Clues

Look for contextual clues. An answer can be right but not the correct answer. The contextual clues will help you find the answer that is most right and is correct. Understand the context in which a phrase or statement is made. This will help you make important distinctions.

Don't Panic

Panicking will not answer any questions for you; therefore, it isn't helpful. When you first see the question, if your mind goes blank, take a deep breath. Force yourself to mechanically go through the steps of solving the problem using the strategies you've learned.

Pace Yourself

Don't get clock fever. It's easy to be overwhelmed when you're looking at a page full of questions, your mind is full of random thoughts and feeling confused, and the clock is ticking down faster than you would like. Calm down and maintain the pace that you have set for yourself. As long as you are on track by monitoring your pace, you are guaranteed to have enough time for yourself. When you get to the last few minutes of the test, it may seem like you won't have enough time left, but if you only have as many questions as you should have left at that point, then you're right on track!

Answer Selection

The best way to pick an answer choice is to eliminate all of those that are wrong, until only one is left and confirm that is the correct answer. Sometimes though, an answer choice may immediately look right. Be careful! Take a second to make sure that the other choices are not equally obvious. Don't make a hasty mistake. There are only two times that you should stop before checking other answers. First is when you are positive that the answer choice you have selected is correct. Second is when time is almost out and you have to make a quick guess!

Check Your Work

Since you will probably not know every term listed and the answer to every question, it is important that you get credit for the ones that you do know. Don't miss any questions through careless mistakes. If at all possible, try to take a second to look back over your answer selection and make sure you've selected the correct answer choice and haven't made a costly careless mistake (such as marking an answer choice that you didn't mean to mark). The time it takes for this quick double check should more than pay for itself in caught mistakes.

Beware of Directly Quoted Answers

Sometimes an answer choice will repeat word for word a portion of the question or reference section. However, beware of such exact duplication. It may be a trap! More than likely, the correct choice will paraphrase or summarize a point, rather than being exactly the same wording.

Slang

Scientific sounding answers are better than slang ones. An answer choice that begins "To compare the outcomes..." is much more likely to be correct than one that begins "Because some people insisted..."

Extreme Statements

Avoid wild answers that throw out highly controversial ideas that are proclaimed as established fact. An answer choice that states the "process should used in certain situations, if..." is much more likely to be correct than one that states the "process should be discontinued completely." The first is a calm rational statement and doesn't even make a definitive, uncompromising stance, using a hedge word "if" to provide wiggle room, whereas the second choice is a radical idea and far more extreme.

Answer Choice Families

When you have two or more answer choices that are direct opposites or parallels, one of them is usually the correct answer. For instance, if one answer choice states "x increases" and another answer choice states "x decreases" or "y increases," then those two or three answer choices are very similar in construction and fall into the same family of answer choices. A family of answer choices consists of two or three answer choices, very similar in construction, but often with directly opposite meanings. Usually the correct answer choice will be in that family of answer choices. The "odd man out" or answer choice that doesn't seem to fit the parallel construction of the other answer choices is more likely to be incorrect.

Special Report: How to Overcome Test Anxiety

The very nature of tests caters to some level of anxiety, nervousness, or tension, just as we feel for any important event that occurs in our lives. A little bit of anxiety or nervousness can be a good thing. It helps us with motivation, and makes achievement just that much sweeter. However, too much anxiety can be a problem, especially if it hinders our ability to function and perform.

"Test anxiety," is the term that refers to the emotional reactions that some test-takers experience when faced with a test or exam. Having a fear of testing and exams is based upon a rational fear, since the test-taker's performance can shape the course of an academic career. Nevertheless, experiencing excessive fear of examinations will only interfere with the test-taker's ability to perform and chance to be successful.

There are a large variety of causes that can contribute to the development and sensation of test anxiety. These include, but are not limited to, lack of preparation and worrying about issues surrounding the test.

Lack of Preparation

Lack of preparation can be identified by the following behaviors or situations:

Not scheduling enough time to study, and therefore cramming the night before the test or exam
Managing time poorly, to create the sensation that there is not enough time to do everything
Failing to organize the text information in advance, so that the study material consists of the entire text and not simply the pertinent information
Poor overall studying habits

Worrying, on the other hand, can be related to both the test taker, or many other factors around him/her that will be affected by the results of the test. These include worrying about:

Previous performances on similar exams, or exams in general
How friends and other students are achieving
The negative consequences that will result from a poor grade or failure

There are three primary elements to test anxiety. Physical components, which involve the same typical bodily reactions as those to acute anxiety (to be discussed below). Emotional factors have to do with fear or panic. Mental or cognitive issues concerning attention spans and memory abilities.

Physical Signals

There are many different symptoms of test anxiety, and these are not limited to mental and emotional strain. Frequently there are a range of physical signals that will let a test taker know that he/she is suffering from test anxiety. These bodily changes can include the following:

Perspiring
Sweaty palms
Wet, trembling hands
Nausea
Dry mouth
A knot in the stomach
Headache
Faintness
Muscle tension
Aching shoulders, back and neck
Rapid heart beat
Feeling too hot/cold

To recognize the sensation of test anxiety, a test-taker should monitor him/herself for the following sensations:

The physical distress symptoms as listed above
Emotional sensitivity, expressing emotional feelings such as the need to cry or laugh too much, or a sensation of anger or helplessness
A decreased ability to think, causing the test-taker to blank out or have racing thoughts that are hard to organize or control.

Though most students will feel some level of anxiety when faced with a test or exam, the majority can cope with that anxiety and maintain it at a manageable level. However, those who cannot are faced with a very real and very serious condition, which can and should be controlled for the immeasurable benefit of this sufferer.

Naturally, these sensations lead to negative results for the testing experience. The most common effects of test anxiety have to do with nervousness and mental blocking.

Nervousness

Nervousness can appear in several different levels:

The test-taker's difficulty, or even inability to read and understand the questions on the test
The difficulty or inability to organize thoughts to a coherent form
The difficulty or inability to recall key words and concepts relating to the testing questions (especially essays)
The receipt of poor grades on a test, though the test material was well known by the test taker

Conversely, a person may also experience mental blocking, which involves:

Blanking out on test questions
Only remembering the correct answers to the questions when the test has already finished.

Fortunately for test anxiety sufferers, beating these feelings, to a large degree, has to do with proper preparation. When a test taker has a feeling of preparedness, then anxiety will be dramatically lessened.

The first step to resolving anxiety issues is to distinguish which of the two types of anxiety are being suffered. If the anxiety is a direct result of a lack of preparation, this should be considered a normal reaction, and the anxiety level (as opposed to the test results) shouldn't be anything to worry about. However, if, when adequately prepared, the test-taker still panics, blanks out, or seems to overreact, this is not a fully rational reaction. While this can be considered normal too, there are many ways to combat and overcome these effects.

Remember that anxiety cannot be entirely eliminated, however, there are ways to minimize it, to make the anxiety easier to manage. Preparation is one of the best ways to minimize test anxiety. Therefore the following techniques are wise in order to best fight off any anxiety that may want to build.

To begin with, try to avoid cramming before a test, whenever it is possible. By trying to memorize an entire term's worth of information in one day, you'll be shocking your system, and not giving yourself a very good chance to absorb the information. This is an easy path to anxiety, so for those who suffer from test anxiety, cramming should not even be considered an option.

Instead of cramming, work throughout the semester to combine all of the material which is presented throughout the semester, and work on it gradually as the course goes by, making sure to master the main concepts first, leaving minor details for a week or so before the test.

To study for the upcoming exam, be sure to pose questions that may be on the examination, to gauge the ability to answer them by integrating the ideas from your texts, notes and lectures, as well as any supplementary readings.

If it is truly impossible to cover all of the information that was covered in that particular term, concentrate on the most important portions, that can be covered very well. Learn these concepts as best as possible, so that when the test comes, a goal can be made to use these concepts as presentations of your knowledge.

In addition to study habits, changes in attitude are critical to beating a struggle with test anxiety. In fact, an improvement of the perspective over the entire test-taking experience can actually help a test taker to enjoy studying and therefore improve the overall experience. Be certain not to overemphasize the significance of the grade - know that the result of the test is neither a reflection of self worth, nor is it a measure of intelligence; one grade will not predict a person's future success.

To improve an overall testing outlook, the following steps should be tried:

Keeping in mind that the most reasonable expectation for taking a test is to expect to try to demonstrate as much of what you know as you possibly can.
Reminding ourselves that a test is only one test; this is not the only one, and there will be others.
The thought of thinking of oneself in an irrational, all-or-nothing term should be avoided at all costs.
A reward should be designated for after the test, so there's something to look forward to. Whether it be going to a movie, going out to eat, or simply visiting friends, schedule it in advance, and do it no matter what result is expected on the exam.

Test-takers should also keep in mind that the basics are some of the most important things, even beyond anti-anxiety techniques and studying. Never neglect the basic social, emotional and biological needs, in order to try to absorb information. In order to best achieve, these three factors must be held as just as important as the studying itself.

Study Steps

Remember the following important steps for studying:

Maintain healthy nutrition and exercise habits. Continue both your recreational activities and social pass times. These both contribute to your physical and emotional well being.
Be certain to get a good amount of sleep, especially the night before the test, because when you're overtired you are not able to perform to the best of your best ability.
Keep the studying pace to a moderate level by taking breaks when they are needed, and varying the work whenever possible, to keep the mind fresh instead of getting bored. When enough studying has been done that all the material that can be learned has been learned, and the test taker is prepared for the test, stop studying and do something relaxing such as listening to music, watching a movie, or taking a warm bubble bath.

There are also many other techniques to minimize the uneasiness or apprehension that is experienced along with test anxiety before, during, or even after the examination. In fact, there are a great deal of things that can be done to stop anxiety from interfering with lifestyle and performance. Again, remember that anxiety will not be eliminated entirely, and it shouldn't be. Otherwise that "up" feeling for exams would not exist, and most of us depend on that sensation to perform better than usual. However, this anxiety has to be at a level that is manageable.

Of course, as we have just discussed, being prepared for the exam is half the battle right away. Attending all classes, finding out what knowledge will be expected on the exam, and knowing the exam schedules are easy steps to lowering anxiety. Keeping up with work will remove the need to cram, and efficient study habits will eliminate wasted time. Studying should be done in an ideal location for concentration, so that it is simple to become interested in the material and give it complete attention. A method such as SQ3R (Survey, Question, Read, Recite, Review) is a wonderful key to follow to make sure that the study habits are as effective as possible, especially in the case of learning from a textbook. Flashcards are great techniques for memorization. Learning to take good notes will mean that notes will be full of useful information, so that less sifting will need to be done to seek out what is pertinent for studying. Reviewing notes after class and then again on occasion will keep the information fresh in the mind. From notes that have been taken summary sheets and outlines can be made for simpler reviewing.

A study group can also be a very motivational and helpful place to study, as there will be a sharing of ideas, all of the minds can work together, to make sure that everyone understands, and the studying will be made more interesting because it will be a social occasion.

Basically, though, as long as the test-taker remains organized and self confident, with efficient study habits, less time will need to be spent studying, and higher grades will be achieved.

To become self confident, there are many useful steps. The first of these is "self talk." It has been shown through extensive research, that self-talk for students who suffer from test anxiety, should be well monitored, in order to make sure that it contributes to self confidence as opposed to sinking the student. Frequently the self talk of test-anxious students is negative or self-defeating, thinking that everyone else is smarter and faster, that they always mess up, and that if they don't do well, they'll fail the entire course. It is important to decreasing anxiety that awareness is made of self talk. Try writing any negative self thoughts and then disputing them with a positive statement instead. Begin self-encouragement as though it was a friend speaking. Repeat positive statements to help reprogram the mind to believing in successes instead of failures.

Helpful Techniques

Other extremely helpful techniques include:

Self-visualization of doing well and reaching goals
While aiming for an "A" level of understanding, don't try to "overprotect" by setting your expectations lower. This will only convince the mind to stop studying in order to meet the lower expectations.
Don't make comparisons with the results or habits of other students. These are individual factors, and different things work for different people, causing different results.
Strive to become an expert in learning what works well, and what can be done in order to improve. Consider collecting this data in a journal.
Create rewards for after studying instead of doing things before studying that will only turn into avoidance behaviors.
Make a practice of relaxing - by using methods such as progressive relaxation, self-hypnosis, guided imagery, etc - in order to make relaxation an automatic sensation.
Work on creating a state of relaxed concentration so that concentrating will take on the focus of the mind, so that none will be wasted on worrying.
Take good care of the physical self by eating well and getting enough sleep.
Plan in time for exercise and stick to this plan.

Beyond these techniques, there are other methods to be used before, during and after the test that will help the test-taker perform well in addition to overcoming anxiety.

Before the exam comes the academic preparation. This involves establishing a study schedule and beginning at least one week before the actual date of the test. By doing this, the anxiety of not having enough time to study for the test will be automatically eliminated. Moreover, this will make the studying a much more effective experience, ensuring that the learning will be an easier process. This relieves much undue pressure on the test-taker.

Summary sheets, note cards, and flash cards with the main concepts and examples of these main concepts should be prepared in advance of the actual studying time. A topic should never be eliminated from this process. By omitting a topic because it isn't expected to be on the test is only setting up the test-taker for anxiety should it actually appear on the exam. Utilize the course syllabus for laying out the topics that should be studied. Carefully go over the notes that were made in class, paying special attention to any of the issues that the professor took special care to emphasize while lecturing in class. In the textbooks, use the chapter review, or if possible, the chapter tests, to begin your review.

It may even be possible to ask the instructor what information will be covered on the exam, or what the format of the exam will be (for example, multiple choice, essay, free form, true-false). Additionally, see if it is possible to find out how many questions will be on the test. If a review sheet or sample test has been offered by the professor, make good use of it, above anything else, for the preparation for the test. Another great resource for getting to know the examination is reviewing tests from previous semesters. Use these tests to review, and aim to achieve a 100% score on each of the possible topics. With a few exceptions, the goal that you set for yourself is the highest one that you will reach.

Take all of the questions that were assigned as homework, and rework them to any other possible course material. The more problems reworked, the more skill and confidence will form as a result. When forming the solution to a problem, write out each of the steps. Don't simply do head work. By doing as many steps on paper as possible, much clarification and therefore confidence will be formed. Do this with as many homework problems as possible, before checking the answers. By checking the answer after each problem, a reinforcement will exist, that will not be on the exam. Study situations should be as exam-like as possible, to prime the test-taker's system for the experience. By waiting to check the answers at the end, a psychological advantage will be formed, to decrease the stress factor.

Another fantastic reason for not cramming is the avoidance of confusion in concepts, especially when it comes to mathematics. 8-10 hours of study will become one hundred percent more effective if it is spread out over a week or at least several days, instead of doing it all in one sitting. Recognize that the human brain requires time in order to assimilate new material, so frequent breaks and a span of study time over several days will be much more beneficial.

Additionally, don't study right up until the point of the exam. Studying should stop a minimum of one hour before the exam begins. This allows the brain to rest and put things in their proper order. This will also provide the time to become as relaxed as possible when going into the examination room. The test-taker will also have time to eat well and eat sensibly. Know that the brain needs food as much as the rest of the body. With enough food and enough sleep, as well as a relaxed attitude, the body and the mind are primed for success.

Avoid any anxious classmates who are talking about the exam. These students only spread anxiety, and are not worth sharing the anxious sentimentalities.

Before the test also involves creating a positive attitude, so mental preparation should also be a point of concentration. There are many keys to creating a positive attitude. Should fears become rushing in, make a visualization of taking the exam, doing well, and seeing an A written on the paper. Write out a list of affirmations that will bring a feeling of confidence, such as "I am doing well in my English class," "I studied well and know my material," "I enjoy this class." Even if the affirmations aren't believed at first, it sends a positive message to the subconscious which will result in an alteration of the overall belief system, which is the system that creates reality.

If a sensation of panic begins, work with the fear and imagine the very worst! Work through the entire scenario of not passing the test, failing the entire course, and dropping out of school, followed by not getting a job, and pushing a shopping cart through the dark alley where you'll live. This will place things into perspective! Then, practice deep breathing and create a visualization of the opposite situation - achieving an "A" on the exam, passing the entire course, receiving the degree at a graduation ceremony.

On the day of the test, there are many things to be done to ensure the best results, as well as the most calm outlook. The following stages are suggested in order to maximize test-taking potential:

Begin the examination day with a moderate breakfast, and avoid any coffee or beverages with caffeine if the test taker is prone to jitters. Even people who are used to managing caffeine can feel jittery or light-headed when it is taken on a test day.
Attempt to do something that is relaxing before the examination begins. As last minute cramming clouds the mastering of overall concepts, it is better to use this time to create a calming outlook.
Be certain to arrive at the test location well in advance, in order to provide time to select a location that is away from doors, windows and other distractions, as well as giving enough time to relax before the test begins.
Keep away from anxiety generating classmates who will upset the sensation of stability and relaxation that is being attempted before the exam.
Should the waiting period before the exam begins cause anxiety, create a self-distraction by reading a light magazine or something else that is relaxing and simple.

During the exam itself, read the entire exam from beginning to end, and find out how much time should be allotted to each individual problem. Once writing the exam, should more time be taken for a problem, it should be abandoned, in order to begin another problem. If there is time at the end, the unfinished problem can always be returned to and completed.

Read the instructions very carefully - twice - so that unpleasant surprises won't follow during or after the exam has ended.

When writing the exam, pretend that the situation is actually simply the completion of homework within a library, or at home. This will assist in forming a relaxed atmosphere, and will allow the brain extra focus for the complex thinking function.

Begin the exam with all of the questions with which the most confidence is felt. This will build the confidence level regarding the entire exam and will begin a quality momentum. This will also create encouragement for trying the problems where uncertainty resides.

Going with the "gut instinct" is always the way to go when solving a problem. Second guessing should be avoided at all costs. Have confidence in the ability to do well.

For essay questions, create an outline in advance that will keep the mind organized and make certain that all of the points are remembered. For multiple choice, read every answer, even if the correct one has been spotted - a better one may exist.

Continue at a pace that is reasonable and not rushed, in order to be able to work carefully. Provide enough time to go over the answers at the end, to check for small errors that can be corrected.

Should a feeling of panic begin, breathe deeply, and think of the feeling of the body releasing sand through its pores. Visualize a calm, peaceful place, and include all of the sights, sounds and sensations of this image. Continue the deep breathing, and take a few minutes to continue this with closed eyes. When all is well again, return to the test.

If a "blanking" occurs for a certain question, skip it and move on to the next question. There will be time to return to the other question later. Get everything done that can be done, first, to guarantee all the grades that can be compiled, and to build all of the confidence possible. Then return to the weaker questions to build the marks from there.

Remember, one's own reality can be created, so as long as the belief is there, success will follow. And remember: anxiety can happen later, right now, there's an exam to be written!

After the examination is complete, whether there is a feeling for a good grade or a bad grade, don't dwell on the exam, and be certain to follow through on the reward that was promised…and enjoy it! Don't dwell on any mistakes that have been made, as there is nothing that can be done at this point anyway.

Additionally, don't begin to study for the next test right away. Do something relaxing for a while, and let the mind relax and prepare itself to begin absorbing information again.

From the results of the exam - both the grade and the entire experience, be certain to learn from what has gone on. Perfect studying habits and work some more on confidence in order to make the next examination experience even better than the last one.

Learn to avoid places where openings occurred for laziness, procrastination and day dreaming.

Use the time between this exam and the next one to better learn to relax, even learning to relax on cue, so that any anxiety can be controlled during the next exam. Learn how to relax the body. Slouch in your chair if that helps. Tighten and then relax all of the different muscle groups, one group at a time, beginning with the feet and then working all the way up to the neck and face. This will ultimately relax the muscles more than they were to begin with. Learn how to breathe deeply and comfortably, and focus on this breathing going in and out as a relaxing thought. With every exhale, repeat the word "relax."

As common as test anxiety is, it is very possible to overcome it. Make yourself one of the test-takers who overcome this frustrating hindrance.

Additional Bonus Material

Due to our efforts to try to keep this book to a manageable length, we've created a link that will give you access to all of your additional bonus material.

Please visit http://www.mometrix.com/bonus948/texesbtlplspa to access the information.